HEAVEN

LETTERS TO HEAVEN

MICHELE CYNTHIA BELL

Dear Heaven

2020 White Bird Publications, LLC

Published in the United States
by White Bird Publications, LLC, Texas
www.whitebirdpublications.com

ISBN 978-1-63363-491-6
eBook ISBN 978-1-63363-492-3
Library of Congress Control Number: 2020949565

PRINTED IN THE UNITED STATES OF AMERICA

CONTENTS

i

Remembered on the hardwood

Friends and family pay tribute to the life of Nick Bell

By John Miele
Friday, March 3, 2006

It was a night that the late Nick Bell would have been proud to have seen, as all of his friends paid tribute to him on the basketball court at Eastchester High School. With everyone bringing a competitive edge and a chance to shed

a tear on the hardwood, his friends and family found comfort to see the impact that Nick made on his local community.

Jacqueline Rank believed that Nick's memory felt the need to be preserved and she did so with a night of basketball.

Nick Bell passed away after a five-year battle with bone cancer - Ewing's sarcoma on Dec. 29, 2005.

"Nick got cancer from playing basketball," said Rank. "Even after he got

Nick Bell would have been proud to see his friends and family pay tribute to his legacy.

see Nick Bell page 15

ii

SPOTLIGHT

Bell bounces back from battle with cancer

By Danny Lopriore

The words tumor, cancer and "Ewing's sarcoma" meant nothing to 14-year-old Nicholas Bell – until the chemotherapy began.

"The chemo was horrible and I knew right then with that first treatment it wasn't good," said Bell, who was diagnosed with cancer in November of 2001 after finding a big lump on his knee. "I thought I had pulled a muscle or something while I was playing basketball. But when my mother, grandmother and the doctor told me it was a tumor (bone cancer), it got serious."

Getting serious began with a biopsy, followed by weeks of radiation and chemotherapy to shrink the tumor that had grown to the size of a softball, then surgery to remove it. The ensuing year was marked with week-long therapy sessions that would leave Bell filled with nauseating cancer-killing chemicals and days of non-stop sleep during recovery.

"You get three weeks off and then a week in the hospital for chemo," Bell said. "I would sleep non-stop for like six days. Then I'd want to eat everything. I guess I just went day to day. Sometimes I would tell my mother I didn't want to do the chemo sessions but she, my grandmother and some of my mentors, who were also going through chemo, pushed me to keep going."

School was out of the question during the year of chemotherapy and when his doctors released him to return to Eastchester High School in January, Bell, who claims he would rather play ball than do homework, was thrilled to go back to class.

"You had to ask the kids who came to visit me at home during the time I was out," Bell said. "Everyone came. Kids I didn't really know that well visited me. They really supported me. That's why I'd like to do something like help other kids with cancer. It really means a lot to have people encouraging you."

Aside from his mother Michelle Bell, a single mom, younger sister Bianca and other family members, Nicholas got some extra inspiration

from friends he met during his hospital stays and therapy sessions. Several of them, including his friend from Florida, Pablo, shared lost hair, sickness, weakness and fears.

"Pablo would joke with me and have a good time, but he would also set me straight when I would take things too lightly," Bell said. "He's a little older and recently lost his leg when his cancer returned. He keeps me going and tells me never to give up or get down. Having people who are going through the same thing helps a lot."

The scars of Bell's ordeal during this recent phase of recovery are more physical than emotional, thanks to his positive attitude and help from his family and friends. He even jokes with people who notice the foot-long scar on his leg where the tumor was removed and the roundish mark on his chest where the chemotherapy portal was inserted.

"I tell kids the scar on my leg is from a shark attack and the one on my chest is a bullet wound," Bell laughed. "You know, they believe it until I tell them the real story."

As for school, Bell is glad to be

back in the hallways and classrooms, but still doesn't love the work. He favors English among his subjects and hopes to write a little about his experiences with cancer when he gets up the courage to sit down and reflect.

"I'd like to write a book maybe," Bell said. "I'd like to tell people about what it was to go through it. It might help some other kid who has to face it. I might also want to become a psychologist, to get to know how people think and to help them."

For now, Nicholas, who is not allowed to participate in contact or physically demanding sports like basketball or football, enjoys collecting his favorite athletic shoes and hats. He has a closet full of all kinds of sneakers.

"He has so many shoes," Bianca Bell said. "Piles of them. He's a maniac about shoes."

Nick Bell replied, "I just have to match (my clothes). The hats are just a thing I like."

Bell knows he has to protect himself from injury that might cause a recurrence of the cancer, but he would love to get back on the basketball court, where he spent many years de-

veloping his game in Eastchester recreation programs.

"I'd love to be a coach someday," Bell said. "Maybe I could help with the school basketball team or something like that. I could really help by showing that you can work hard and win, even with cancer."

His experience has also given him opportunities to inform and educate. The Bell family, which has been involved in various cancer support and fund-raising efforts, has also established its own a children's cancer fund called, "Skipper's Angel Wings", to help other kids deal with the disease and the treatment.

"Dr. Aaron Rausen, Nick's doctor and a top oncologist at NYU, has had Nick speak to medical students about his experience with cancer and he's done a good job," Michelle Bell said. "I think his attitude and courage have helped him grow."

Young Nick is certain his "childhood" is over.

"I guess I was forced to grow up," Bell said. "Now I have to mature in school and get ready for college. I want to live a long life and do good things."

For information on "Skipper's Angels Wings" call 771-8710.

For more information

Eastchester High School sophomore Nicholas Bell sits with a collection of his favorite shoes and caps. Bell, who recently completed a year of cancer treatment and underwent major surgery, is hoping to help other young people who are stricken with cancer.

Ewing's sarcoma is named after Dr. James Ewing who described the tumor in the 1920s. It is a cancer which can develop anywhere in the body most usually occurs in the teenage years. It usually starts in a bone, most commonly in one of the bones of the hips, upper arm or thigh. Although often thought of as a bone tumor, this condition can develop in the soft tissue near bones. In most cases the cause is unknown.

The most common symptom a child has when this cancer develops is pain in the bone where the tumor is located. There may eventually be some swelling in the area and it may become tender to touch. Occasionally the child develops a fever.

Danny Lopriore/Review Press

Nicola Bell, inspiration for Skipper's Angel Wings, dies

Tuckahoe boy, 18, fought brave battle against bone cancer

Ken Valenti
The Journal News

TUCKAHOE — Nicola "Skipper" Bell, the teenager whose fight with cancer led his mother to create an organization to help other children and teenagers battling the disease, has died.

The 18-year-old died at home, which was his wish, said his mother, Michele Bell.

"He was very, very respectful," she said. "He had a vast amount of respect. He never asked for pity. . . . He always worried about everybody else, right up until his last breath. And to his last breath, he said, 'Mom, I love you. I'm going home.'"

He died Dec. 29 and services were held yesterday at Ferncliff

Cemetery in Hartsdale.

The teen, who went by "Nick" or "Nicky," was well known through out Eastchester, his mother said.

"He was extremely loved and admired by the entire community," she said.

At the age of 14, while a freshman at Eastchester High School, he was diagnosed with Ewing's Sarcoma, a form of bone cancer, when doctors found a tumor in his leg.

In 2003, his mother, having lost a job because she needed time to care for her son, began Skipper's Angel Wings.

Through his chemotherapy, blood transfusions and hospital stays, Bell was not alone. His grandmother, Barbara Feyl, drove weekly from Albany to see him, from before the time he was diag-

nosed.

Bell inspired a classmate among his friends, who stood by him, said family friend Yolanda Delarosa. And a support group of four women — his mother, Delarosa and Ann Marie DeCaruso — saw him throughout his ordeal.

"There was nothing we would not have done for that boy," Delarosa said. "Not a thing."

In recent days, his friends lifted his wheelchair into a van to take him to the Galleria mall, Delarosa said. There, he bought a North Face jacket, a cap and sneakers. Always on the forefront of fashion, he owned hundreds of pairs of sneakers, his mother said.

He also had his photograph taken with his mother and Santa Claus.

A Catholic, he was "very, very spiritual," Delarosa said.

He was born June 25, 1987, in Niskayuna, N.Y., to Michele Bell and Nicola Mele.

"He is survived by his mother of Tuckahoe and his father of Albany, two sisters, Bonita-Marisa Bell and Isabella Mele, both of Albany; his grandmother, Barbara Feyl, and many aunts, uncles and cousins.

Funeral arrangements were handled by the Westchester Funeral Home in Eastchester.

Donations in his name may be made to Skipper's Angel Wings Children's Cancer Fund, P.O. Box 206 Eastchester, NY 10709.

"I tell you this kid was the best," Delarosa said. "And he will never be forgotten."

Reach Ken Valenti at kvalenti@thejournalnews.com or (914) 696-8258.

Nicola "Skipper" Bell

Farewell to a brave teen

Family, friends remember Nicola Bell, who lost his fight with cancer.

were held yesterday at Ferncliff   from before the time he was diag-   and Nicola Mele.

Dear Heaven

Nick Bell
June 20, 1987 – December 29, 2005
AN UNFORGETTABLE MAN

Original letters were written shortly after Nicky died.
His legacy of love will always be etched within our mind,
body, and spirit forever.

With Family and Friends

*I want to thank all the readers who wanted to
see my son's life memorialized within these pages.*

Nick Bell
6-20-1987 — 12-29-2005

This memorial was created in the memory of Nick Bell. He was born in New York on June 20, 1987, and passed away on December 29, 2005, at the age of 18 after a five-year battle with Ewing's Sarcoma.

Photos by Stuart Bayer/The Journal News
Nick Bell with his mom, Michelle of Eastchester, in his room at New York University Medical Center. Nick is suffering from Ewing's Sarcoma and is recovering from surgery last week to remove a tumor from his right fibula.

x

None of these letters and correspondences have been edited to change them in any way. So be aware there are the normal, original typos, from people just writing with their hearts.

ABOUT NICK BELL

"Graced with Your Presence"

My son's legacy began the moment of his conception. As I carried him for nine beautiful months, I sang or hummed to Nicky every night as he was growing in my tummy and thanked God for his gift. Nicky never took life for granted; he was a pure soul who loved so graciously.

Our bond was unconditional from the moment he was born, as the nurse placed him upon my stomach on June 20, 1987, Nicky looked dagger into my eyes. I knew, at that moment, he was a unique soul. He never left my hip until the very end, on December 29, 2005. For eighteen years, we were loyal to one another. Nicky gave me the meaning of life. I have no right to expect, nor will anyone ever take that from me. Nicky was a charismatic soul, always worried about others. He never showed pity or concession for what God had in store for him. Although life threw him a curveball, he exuded happiness with his infectious smile.

His friends and family were blessed to know Nicky. They loved and adored him immensely with their undying love until the end. Everyone that was graced with his presence admired his passion and fight for life, his wisdom, his hardy laugh, and, most of all, his incredible patience.

He projected a strong sense of how life should be lived to those around him through his faith, love, and respect. "Please," "Can I," "Thank you," and "I love you" were a small part of his daily vocabulary. He always had the utmost respect for everyone he met, never greedy, needy, or disloyal. Nicky was a peaceful soul. He never entertained chaos in his life.

God called for him because of his purity. There are times I

feel guilty that I brought Nicky into this cruel world. Yet, after I ponder those thoughts, I comfort my broken heart and say, "I am proud to have had a son that illuminated presence to those lives he touched."

Thank you, Nicky, for teaching me patience. My life since you has been with God. It has been slightly alleviated of loneliness to know that God is holding you in his arms and welcomed you into heaven. I know we will meet again one day.

"Mom, I love you. I'm going home," were the last words he spoke between his tiny breaths before God took my son.

I love you, Nicky.
Mommy

TRIBUTES & CONDOLENCES

FRIENDS

NICK WILL LIVE ON IN THE HEARTS AND SOULS OF EACH ONE OF HIS FRIENDS forever. Love never dies. God bless you all. Sincerely sorry for the loss of Nick. Blessings from NJ friends of angel Mark C. Fearon

HAPPY MOM'S DAY

To Nick's MOM — Have a Blessed Mother's Day. Remember, Nick is never very far. He walks beside you every day. Fill the cracks in your broken heart with memories of Nick & celebrate the wonderful child born to you — NICK. This Mother's Day, honor him by being happy. The ones we love in heaven want us to smile. So give Nick a big smile like only a mom can give!

FRIENDS

You will NEVER BE FORGOTTEN.
Love to YOU, NICK.
Let your friends feel you near.

SO SORRY FOR YOUR LOSS

THANK YOU FOR MY LIFE.
Bless You. I Love YOU.

SO LOVED
R.I.P. Nick

WHAT A SMILE. NICK LIGHTS UP THE HEAVENS NOW!
Just the look in each other's eyes can tell what a wonderful mother and son relationship you had! God bless you and RIP, Nick. It ain't the end. No goodbyes. Its "I will see you later, my son!
Maria, Daughter Of Mrika Gjelaj - passerby

ANOTHER ONE FOR A SPECIAL LOVING MOM WITH SON!
I can see where Nick got his looks. God bless him. RIP! And the Lord said, *I will wipe away all the tears. He who believeth in me will have eternal life!*
Maria Daughter of Mrika Gjelaj - Passerby

MY DEAREST NICKY, MY SON
MICHELE - MOMMY

DEAR NICKY,

LET ME TRY TO DESCRIBE THE GIFT THAT YOU HAVE GIVEN TO ME. YOUR arrival eighteen years ago was unmistakably marked with anxious trepidation.

The journey you undertook was not of a scheduled nature, but more of God's will.

By far, the finest creative gift was you—for when you emerged into my world, I became reborn with my heart so willing to share its wealth.

There you were, a small wonder, a tiny reflection of combined traits that would ultimately be recreated into the distinctive person you have become.

I never realized that my heart was so willing to share so much love with a stranger so small and needy. You didn't arrive with instructions

It was strictly learning as you go.

I remember the first time you crawled.

It wasn't until that one day, totally unexpected that you did it all by yourself.

From then on, it seemed to get a little bit easier since you had this great disposition.

And that smile that went all the way across your beautiful face. You had a little sister on the way.

And you became that special big brother that you turned out to be. Sharing and loving was not something that you had to learn.

Even at that young age, you became the teacher. Ever so patient, so caring, so you.

As you grew, you obtained a wonderful gift of laughter.

I offered you the tools to learn and trust and to be a confident person. You showed me that you could be an independent person.

That day you climbed on to the enormous, yellow school bus for the first time.

You looked so small, yet so ready to embark upon a new venture. It rolled down the street as the tears rolled down my cheeks.

Not because I was sad but because a new chapter in your life was beginning.

You are an intelligent, sensible, affectionate, and sympathetic person, who always seemed to be there for those whose lives you touch.

You have an extraordinary enthusiasm and passion for learning.

You have the ability to communicate your innermost thoughts where so many your age do not.

I am blessed for that.

Now, you are gone physically.

But I know that you are beside me day and night just as I was beside you from the moment you were born till your last breath on this earth.

I never thought that I would look up to someone your age, but that has become evident.

The stranger that entered my life not so long ago has certainly been transformed into a young man.

That I am proud to call... My son. I will never let you go...

Michele — Mommy

WHILE WE ARE APART, I WILL HOLD YOU IN MY HEART AND NEVER LET YOU GO

Distance may separate us,
But my heart will never let you go,
For I carry a part of you with me always.
It keeps me going through the day.
It brings a smile to my face and tears to my eyes.
It is a part of my dreams that I live for and cherish.
That part is my wish,
My only one wish,
To see you again soon.
I know that wish will someday come true, but for now, I
Will hold in my heart
The memory of you and never let you go.
Lovingly, Mommy

MOTHER & SON
A Bond Not Even Death Can Break...
Mom & Nick a love so evident...god bless you Michele so sorry you lost your handsome son, he's not really gone he will live on forever in your heart.

HAPPY MOMS DAY
love YOU ~ MOM

I'LL BE WAITING
Cheers. NEVER SAY GOODBYE. JUST SEE YA LATER

SO
THE GIRLS THEY LOVE HANDSOME NICK...

MISS YOU NICK
you will forever live on in our hearts

WE MISS & LOVE YOU
RIP NICK. You sure are HANDSOME!!!!

TOO YOUNG TO LOSE
Patricia Dufour - passing through
So sad to lose a son at such a young age. I don't know how you bear it. My heart will cry for your loss as I deal with my own.
Peace be with you...
Patricia

MY HEART IS SO SAD
FOR MY SISTER MICHELE

I ONLY MET NICK A FEW TIMES, YEARS AGO, WAY BACK IN 1991. HE WAS JUST a little boy when I found out I had a sister, nephew, and niece. I spent the weekend with my sister Michele. Looking at Nick, I said, "Wow, he is so special." There is such a strong resemblance to Nick and my son and my other nephews. Michele brought the kids down to meet their uncle and other cousins for the first time the following weekend, and that was it. Life lost touch. I longed to find my sister again.

My family and I moved back to New York, but I never stopped looking for my sister Michele and her kids. I tried everything. I prayed about it for years. In February of 2007, I believe God answered. I sat at my computer all day looking up the same way I had for years. I think God put new info online for me to locate her finally. I read online through the course of finding her about Nicky's illness. I was now frantic to find her and help her out with him.

When I finally met up with Rick, her boyfriend online, the first question I asked was, "How's Nicky." With sad disappointment, I was told he didn't make it. Oh, my heart cried out for Michele. I believe things happen for a reason, and things happen at the time they do. Even though I wish so much I could have been part of there family and watching Nicky grow up. It didn't happen. All I can do now is be there for

Michele, my sister. I know that Nicky was an amazing person. Thru the pic's and thru learning from his mom and thru just knowing if the resemblance is so strong with my son and my other nephews in looks, then also through his

9

heart, he resembles us, which is having a good heart. My heart yearns just to meet him one more time and not take him for granted. Which we all have done and one time or another. You never know what might happen to anyone, so you should never take anyone for granted. You should never assume that that person will always be there.

We need to live in the moment and enjoy who we have now and never think that it will always be there when we need them. You never know what's around the corner and where our lives will take us. Love and be loved without any hesitation. Live life as if it were your last day. Now still not satisfied of ever knowing Nicky more than I did. I will be there for Michele and never take her for granted and hope never to lose her again. My heart is so sad for her. I can not even imagine what it feel's like to lose your own child. Our children are supposed to bury their parents, not the other way around. As I tell Michele, it is not the end of Nicky. She will see him again and that she just needs to have patience and wait for the Glorious day.

KIM BELL – AUNT

CONDOLENCES

SO SORRY
Tina - passer-by

Michelle,
I can not even begin to imagine the pain you have gone through. I only know how hard it is to lose a parent. My dad passed away Aug 13th from a two-year battle with lung cancer. He lived a much longer life than Nicky, but I dare not say a fuller one because it sounds as though Nicky lived a good full life from havng you as a MOM. My heart sank when I read when he past away as my birthday is Dec 29th so I feel as though I have a guardian angel looking out for me. Hopefully my Dad is looking out for Nicky now that he is there with him as he did not like to see kids suffer in any way. I have a 21 yr old and can not imagine my life without him. May you find peace in your heart knowing that he is not suffering any more. Feel free to email me anytime. You can reach me through my Dad's web page http://thomaskliguori.memory-of.com
Take care. Tina

SORRY FOR YOUR LOSS.
Nicole - visitor

I am sooo sorry for your loss. It seems NICK was definately a blessing to have in your life. Never forget your memories and hold them close to your heart. It brings tears of happiness to my eyes to see what a wonderful relationship you guys had. I am sure Nick is all around you and your family. My thoughts and prayers are with you. God Bless You all now and always. Nick was very lucky to have a mom like you.

QUEST FOR LIFE
Philamina - Friend from Lourdes

MICHELE, YOU HAVE CREATED A BEAUTIFUL TRIBUTE TO YOUR SON NICK; well deserved for such a special person. I met you, Nick (then 17), and his grandmother Barbara on his last and final trip to Lourdes. I went to Lourdes to find a healing for myself - I found that at Lourdes and with meeting Nick and having the pleasure to have my mind, body and soul healed by Mother Mary and her angel Nick. I learned more from observing the faith, strength, courage, zest for life and compassion for others that Nick naturally conveyed just by being with him each day.

His quest for life never ended; Nick had something to give with each breath of his life and I had the pleasure and blessings to witness his grace and kind humble soul. I keep a picture of him on my mirror and pray to him whenever I need strength for the day or for whatever trial I'm facing. Nick is with me each day since I met him. I was 55 years old when I met Nick with children and grandchildren of my own and Nick brought me to a place in my heart and soul that healed some of the scars, wounds, fears and anxiety in my life that I faced on a daily basis. He is an angel in my life and I will never forget him, his life, grandmother Barbara and yourself for sharing this great gift.

When I close my eyes and think of Nick I see that wonderful smile of his. God didn't skimp one bit when he created Nick, (body and soul). I went to Lourdes the following summer after Nick's passing with his grandmother Barbara. We prayed for Nick and thought of him each step of our journey. I know Nick is in heaven, and watching over his friends and family. That's just Nick!!!!!!

Love and compassion for to those who know and loved Nick.

MY GRANDSON — I MISS YOU, SKIPPER
BARBARA - Grandmother
MY DEAREST SKIPPER, MY LOVE & MY PRAYERS ARE TO YOU EVERY DAY. WE HAVE THE BEST MEMORIES, AND YOU ARE HERE WITH ME...

MEMORIAL TRIBUTES

MICHELE BELL ON MAY 3, 2007
NICKY, YOUR MEMORY BEGINS WHEN I CONCEIVED YOU, MY FIRST CHILD. I was blessed from above. Love, Mommy

---

AUNT KIM LIVINGSTON ON MAY 3, 2007
Nicky I regret not getting the chance to be a part of your short life Till we meet again. Love Aunt kim and cousins

---

LISA PERFETTI ON MAY 3, 2007
Nicky, Sorry I missed meeting you in person. Keep watching over your Mom who misses you dearly. Peace, Lisa

---

RHONDA ENGELS JAWOR WIFE OF BILL JAWOR ON MAY 3, 2007
My deepest sympathy for the loss of your handsome son. God bless you.

YVONNE-THE LOVE OF ANGEL DOUGLAS SAGER ON MAY 3, 2007
Nicky,Thinking of you and your loving family who miss you so much.God Bless

---

JUDY OF CHARLES WILDHAGEN ON MAY 3, 2007

Nothing can ever take away the love a heart holds dear, fond memories linger everyday, Remembrances keeps them near xox

SELMA FLYNN ON MAY 3, 2007

heaven in your heart starlight in your soul,angels in your life today and always god bless you my angels john.bobbo ˆjˆ

NINON ON MAY 4, 2007

I was deeply touched by the beautiful photos...please accept my deepest sympathies, from Quebec.

A PASSERBY ON MAY 4, 2007

Your son was a very beautiful young man. I am so sorry for your loss. xx

MARTHA SCOTT GM SAMANTHA SCOTT ON MAY 4, 2007

The pain of the loss of a child is always hard to cope with. May God bless.

FAMILY OF WILLIAM MYERS ON MAY 4, 2007

May God guide you and give you strength on this journey & keep you in His loving care close to Him always

CINDY NIXON ON MAY 4, 2007

I didn't know your son but you have made such a sweet tribute to him, i feel your pain, god bless you and yours!

LARAINE MOM TO ANGEL CYNTHIA HERNANDEZ ON MAY 4, 2007
Memories of u will 4ever stay in our hearts, u are so loved precious Nick, u are the sunshine in everyone's heart.

NANCY - MOM TO ANGEL MIRANDA BARNES ON MAY 4, 2007
Good morning and lighting a candle for a special angel.

HELEN - SIS TO ANGEL - MICHAEL FLISSIKOWSKI ON MAY 4, 2007
HANDSOME ANGEL NICK SEND HUGS ON THE WIND, TO LET MUM NO YOUR NOT FAR AWAY, GOD BLESS

RACHEL MUMMY OF- JAYDEN WEEKES-MCKIE ON MAY 4, 2007
im so sorry for your loss,all my love i send to you nick and all of your family xxxxxxxxxxxxx

---

ANGELA MCKERNAN PAUL'S MUM ON MAY 4, 2007
my heart feels your pain,so sorry for the loss of your handsome son.sending love to you both xxx

---

JANE EISELE ON MAY 4, 2007
Blessed Nicky, you are so loved and missed. Shine your heavenly light on your mother. God Bless.

ONESIMA - MOM TO ANGEL DINO RAPONI ON MAY 5, 2007

Angel Nick your light will shine 4ever in ur Mom's heart. God bless precious. Hugs & kisses.

TINA MCCARTY AUNT TO ANGIE-ROBERT ON MAY 5, 2007

Never knew Nick but yr tribute is so touching, I feel like I have met your son. Wrap yr angel wings around yr mom 4ever

---

MOM OF JONATHAN BREWER ON MAY 5, 2007

Once an Angel on Earth & Now an Angel in Heaven. Love to all...

TAMMY MOM TO ANGEL STEFANIE BAKER ON MAY 5, 2007

I am sorry for ur loss of ur handsome Nick. I know my words will never heal ur pain, but u will always be in my prayers.

PEGGY MOM TO ANGEL SHANNON DENISE WITT ON MAY 5, 2007

So sorry for ur loss, I know the pain UR in, God will help you get through this. Prayers for all

---

DIANNE MOM OF ANGEL NICHOLAS WHITE ON MAY 5, 2007

May cherished memories sustain u thru each day & may ur angel's love keep u thou apart until u embrace once again

---

KATHY EDWARDS (MOM OF MICHELLE) ON MAY 6, 2007

God bless U and give U strength. Nick will always B loved & missed. xxoo

DIANE ANGEL MOM- KATIE CASSIDY ON MAY 6, 2007

God Bless each and everyone of you who love and miss your precious Nick!! My heartfelt sympathy!!

LISA PERFETTI ON MAY 6, 2007

Nick, you are truly missed! Keep watching over your Mom like you have been. Hugs, Lisa

DEBRA CELLI ON MAY 6, 2007

Nicky please give Mom courage to be strong, let her feel your presense everyday to guide her. Love you always xoxoxoxo

ELLEN MUM OF ADAM GILMOUR ON MAY 7, 2007

I am so sorry for your loss of your worderful son Nicky.. memories are priceless hugs xxxx

PATRICIA DUFOUR (FFOS) ON MAY 7, 2007

My sympathy for your loss!

NANCY˜MOM TO ANGEL MIRANDA BARNES ON MAY 7, 2007

Lighting this candle and saying prayers for your family.

DENISE MUM TO ANGEL JAMES KNEALE ON MAY 7, 2007
We shall find peace. We shall hear angels, we shall see the sky sparkling with diamonds." xxx

---

DENISE, MOM TO ANGEL REBECCA SMITH ON MAY 7, 2007
be with your Mom this Mother's Day, Nick, just as my Rebecca is by my side, show us your presence.

KELLY TARR ON MAY 7, 2007
What a beautiful beautiful young man! Rest well, Nick!

LISA SIS TO MATT JONES ON MAY 7, 2007
Nicky, shine your light down on your Mom & let her feel the warmth of your love. God Bless. RIP.

JACKY-PASSERBY ON MAY 7, 2007
You were the light in your mothers life. Please continue to shine on her so she will know you are fine.

JACKY-PASSERBY ON MAY 7, 2007
I'm sorry for the pain that your loved ones had to endure. Sleep Well. When I go I hope to meet you up there.

SHELLY ALWAYSKENNYSMOM ON MAY 7, 2007
Im so very sorry for your loss of precious Nick.I wish U much strength 4 today, tomorrow & always...XXOO

LISA PERFETTI ON MAY 8, 2007

Nick, you are missed! God Bless you and your Mom. Keep watching over your Mom. Peace, Lisa

---

LISA TAQUINO ON MAY 8, 2007

Thinking of you Nicky and your family. May God bless you all.

LINDA MOM OF MICHAEL ARRIGO ON MAY 8, 2007

YOU'RE LIKE A SUNBEAM LIGHTING UP LIFE'S GARDEN. YOU ARE IN MY PRAYERS.

DIANNE MOM OF ANGEL NICHOLAS WHITE ON MAY 8, 2007

May you have cherished memories to sustain you, a heart filled with love & your angel forever by your side

---

LISA DAUGHTER OF DAVID H. MULLIGAN ON MAY 8, 2007

I am so sorry about your beautiful son. You are in my thoughts. Love Lisa.

YVONNE THE LOVE OF ANGEL DOUG SAGER ON MAY 8, 2007

Good-Night Nicky send Angel kisses to your mom who misses you so much. God Bless

---

JUDY OF CHARLES WILDHAGEN ON MAY 9, 2007

Thinking of you and your family, sending hugs to all who love and miss you xoxox

---

BONNIE PASSER BY ON MAY 9, 2007

Iam so very sad for you. Jesus had bigger plans for him. God Speed Nick

---

PAMELA (DAUGHTER OF ALVARO D. CARVALHO) ON MAY 9, 2007

So sorry 4 ur loss.Nick is very handsome & appears 2 have lived a good life.May u take comfort in that.God bless u all

---

RHONDA CRAIG SEHON'S MOM ON MAY 9, 2007

Lighting a candle in memory of Nick. May his memory burn 4ever in the hearts and minds of those that loved him

---

WITH LOVE FROM IRAQ ANGEL ABEER HAMZA ON, MAY 10, 2007

SENDING LOVE FROM HEAVEN TO YOUR FAMILY

ANGEL ALEC KRUGER ON MAY 10, 2007

BLOWING KISSES FROM HEAVEN TO U FAMILY

RENEE GRINOLDS (JAMIE DAWNS MOM) ON MAY 10, 2007

Nick, lighting this candle so that your light may shine brightly forever. God Bless.

BEATRICE A. NY NEIGHBOR ON MAY 10, 2007

I am so sorry for your loss, your son looked like a beautiful person, I hope now he is in peace and watching over you!

TRACI BARNAI MOMMY 2. VANESSA ON MAY 11, 2007

our hearts our like treasure chests full of love and memories. xoxo

ROSE GRAM TO ANGEL BRITTANY SYFERT ON MAY 11, 2007

IN UR MOMENTS OF QUITE REFLECTION,MAY MEMORIES OF ALL U'VE SHARED BE A PART OF GOD'S EMBRACING COMFORT.

LISA PERFETTI ON MAY 11, 2007

Nick, Thank you for doing such a great job watching over your Mom. Keep sending her your love. Peace, Lisa

I MISS YOU SO MUCH ON MAY 12, 2007

This weekend is most difficult my love, my life...you never left me alone on any holiday... MOMMY MISSES YOU XOXOXO

THERESA ON MAY 13, 2007

Dear Nick, You & your Mom are in my thoughts & prayers this Mothers Day. God Bless

ANGIE ON MAY 13, 2007

i was reading ur site nick is a handsome guy sorry 4 ur lost im sure nick is looking down on u today on mothers day.

LISA PERFETTI ON MAY 13, 2007

Nick, we miss you! Keep your Mom safe by continuing to watch over her.

JUDY OF CHARLES WILDHAGEN ON MAY 17, 2007

Just stopping by to say good night angel, watch over your precious family xoxox

---

TINA KESTNER ON MAY 23, 2007

Michele & Nicky you are in my prayers always. Keep watching over your mom. She loves you so much.

DANIELLE REPETTI ON MAY 23, 2007

u took half my heart when u went to heaven. i love u and miss u. thank u for watching us like i knew u would. bff

---

JUDY OF CHARLES ON MAY 23, 2007

You still live on In the hearts and minds, Of the loving family You left behind.

ROSE GRMA TO ANGEL BRITTANY SYFERT ON MAY 23, 2007

PRECIOUS ANGEL, THERE IS NO FEELING MORE COMFORTING & CONSOLING THAN KNOWING U ARE RIGHT NEXT TO UR LOVING FAMILY. XOXO

MOMMY XOXOXO ON MAY 27, 2007
HAPPY MEMORIAL DAY MY LOVE... I MISS YOU
EVERY MINUTE OF THE DAY...:(

MOMMY XOXOXO ON MAY 29, 2007
17 MONTHS HAVE GONE BY WITHOUT BY MY
SIDE... I WONDER WHAT YOU WOULD LOOK LIKE
TODAY... I MISS U MY BABY BOY...

ANGIE ON JUN 5, 2007
i didn't know u but i'm on ur site alot ur mom misses u so
much. i found u from a friends site look over ur mom

AUNT KIM BELL ON JUN 6, 2007
Tears, sadness I have this could be so different you still here
and all of us a family, miss you and never even knew u

JUDY OF CHARLES ON JUN 7, 2007
Forever missed, Forever treasured, Loving you always,
Forgetting you never.

**PARENTS TO ANGEL ~VANESSA BORG~ ON JUN 18,
2007**
Your family is in our prayers, lighting this candle for you
Nick with love to your family from ours. xxx

MOMMY XOXOXO ON JUN 20, 2007
HAPPY 20TH BIRTHDAY MY LOVE... I WISH WE
WERE TOGETHER ON THIS SPECIAL DAY...

AUNT KIM ON JUN 20, 2007

Happy 20th Nicky. from your aunt kim, cousin Kimberly, Zec and Nick

KATHY EDWARDS (MOM OF MICHELLE) ON JUN 23, 2007

Remembering your family Nick as they celebrated your 20th birthday without you. It's so hard. xxoo

MOMMY XOXOXO ON JUL 14, 2007

Nicky... I miss u... I feel u everyday all around me...Luv & Kisses, Mommy

#1 GRAM GRAM ON JUL 18, 2007

LOVING GRANDSON, ALL I CAN SAY IS, I MISS YOU SO MUCH 'SKIPPER'... AND MY LIFE WILL NEVER BE THE SAME!!

SARAH BLAKEWAY JOSHUAS MUMMY ON JUL 20, 2007

thinking of you and your family sending my love x

ILEANA IGNACIORATTARO'S MOM ON JUL 20, 2007

It doesn't matter where are you now, you'll always be in the center of your mom's heart. Sending you my love.

TAMMY~MOM OF ANGELICA HATCHELL ON JUL 20, 2007

Sweet Nick, Keeping your memory in my heart and your family in my thoughts and prayers.

DONNA L~DAUGHTER OF MARLENE BALL ON JUL 20, 2007

Our loved ones are never far away, they are in our hearts and there to stay. Always and forever. God Bless you.

DEBBIE~MUM OF ANGEL STACEY NIGHTINGALE ON JUL 20, 2007

keep sending those signs to your loving family precious Angel Nick. Love and prayers for you all xx

---

MATTHEW BRANDT'S MOM ON JUL 20, 2007

Just passing...What an awesome tribute to your son... Love & Prayers are with You

---

LISA ARCENEAUX TYLER'S MOM ON JUL 20, 2007

Thinking of you Nick and your loved ones. Send angel kisses & hugs to comfort them.

SHELLY ALWAYSKENNYSMOM ON JUL 21, 2007

Thinking of you, Dear Nick & Sending much love 4 mom. XXOO

AUNT KIM LIVINGSTON ON AUG 15, 2007
Thru getting to know you more my heart aches more.

MOMMY NICKY'S MOM ON AUG 15, 2007
Thank you Nicky for watching over Mommy... I miss YOU... Wish you were here to meet your nephews... They adore you...

MOMMY NICKY'S MOM ON AUG 29, 2007
MISSIN U MORE THAN EVER... LUV MOMMY

SHELLY ALWAYSKENNYSMOM ON SEP 13, 2007
I'll B thinking of you today, Sweet Nick... Sending much love 4 mom. XXOO

JONI MOM TO MATHEW ON SEP 13, 2007
Lighting this candle in memory of Nick. My thoughts & prayers are with you & your family.

TAMMY(JACOB'S MOM) BEATY ON SEP 13, 2007
Sending my luv & prayers to u and ur family, what a beautiful young man he is. hugs Tammy

---

LISA ARCENEAUX TYLER'S MOM ON SEP 13, 2007
Thinking of u & ur loved ones. May this candle burn forever in your memory.

JANE, MOM TO SCOTT MATTHEW HILL ON SEP 13, 2007

Here to light a candle in loving memory of Nick and to send love & prayers to his mother who heart is so sad.

CYNTHIA CASTILLO'S AUNT DELIA CARRERA ON SEP 13, 2007

Wishing for peace and comfort for your family, Love Delia Carrera

---

ELLEN MUM OF ADAM GILMOUR ON SEP 13, 2007

Nick thinking of you and your Mom and sending hugs xxx

CRISTINA MOM OF ANGEL EDDY VARGAS ON SEP 13, 2007

God Bless you sweet angel Nick, lighting this candle in your precious memory.

TINA MOM TO ANGEL CARL LITTLEFIELD ON SEP 14, 2007

Lighting this candle for you and your family and wishing you blessings.

DIANE/ MOM TO ANGEL JIMMY BROZZETTI ON SEP 14, 2007

Nick, thinking of u & the many lives u touched. Keeping ur light shining bright & sending love to u & ur loved ones.

DIANE/ MOM TO ANGEL JIMMY BROZZETTI ON SEP 19, 2007

Stopping by to see you handsome angel. You are always in my prayers & thoughts Peace & Love

---

MOMMY MISSING YOU TERRIBLY ON SEP 24, 2007

I feel you all around me... I can feel you...your my inspiration...I wish I could be with you... Mommy

---

DIANE/MOM TO ANGEL JIMMY BROZZETTI ON SEP 28, 2007

So missed So loved As always U will be in my thoughts & prayers. UR family has such a hard long road stay close RIP.."

MOMMY 21 MONTHS GONE BY :(ON SEP 29, 2007

It does not get any easier. I wish u were here to go to dinner with Mommy.

GRAM SKIPPER ON OCT 1, 2007

Nicky, I miss u more & more everday. Your at peace now! I love you, Angels are all around you! See you soon! xxxxoooo

---

DIANE/ MOM TO ANGEL JIMMY BROZZETTI ON OCT 1, 2007

Stopping by to let you know I'm thinking about you and your fami- ly.Sending prayers & love to all God Bless You

---

GRAM I. MISS SOOOO ON OCT 4, 2007

SKIPPER, I'M LISTENING TO YOUR SONGS! Its like u're right here with me, ALLEULIA REALLY LOVE LISTENING TO U'RE SONGS,

DIANE/MOM TO ANGEL JIMMY BROZZETTI ON OCT 9, 2007

May Nick light always shine bright, RIP sweet angel

CAMILLE MOM TO ANGEL FRANCESCO LOCCISANO ON OCT 16, 2007

rest in peace Nicky. My prayers are with you. My son Frankie joined you a month ago. Please hug him from me.

DIANE/MOM TO ANGEL JIMMY BROZZETTI ON OCT 30, 2007

"Hugs & prayers to u & your family precious Angel. Wrap those wings around them & let them feel ur peace

BIANCA MELE ON OCT 31, 2007

i love you <3 i miss you and we will meet again. watch over mike. we love you

DIANE/MOM TO ANGEL JIMMY BROZZETTI ON NOV 9, 2007

Thinking of you Nick and your precious family...keeping you all close to my heart and prayers God Bless

GRAM BABS ON NOV 13, 2007

My dearest Skipper, I love you and u are with me every minute of the day! Your A precious ANGEL

RAYMOND VINCENT ON NOV 13, 2007

I have prayed with your grandmother for you many times. I ask you to now pray for her.

PHILOMENA GOODEVE ON NOV 14, 2007

Nick, God gave you the grace & dignity to carry your cross. Your smile during suffering said it all. Love forever Phil

DIANE/MOM TO ANGEL JIMMY BROZZETTI ON NOV 15, 2007

"Thinking of u & ur family as the holiday season is approaching, Stay close to all who love & misses you God Bless

MOMMY MISSIN U. TERRIBLY ON NOV 23, 2007

It is very lonely everyday and every holiday with out you...Happy Tanksgiv- ing...Gobble Gobble Gobble

LISA PERFETTI ON DEC 2, 2007

Nick, Sending you and your family prayers.

RENEE &. CEDRIC MCCANTS ON DEC 2, 2007

God surely has an angel in his home when he called you. You will be missed but never forgotten. May you rest in peace.

ROSA LAGE ON DEC 3, 2007

Hi Nicky I cant agree more with your moms words. Your love for each other was trully undconditional. I admire you both.

ROSA LAGE ON DEC 3, 2007

I love you and miss you and thank God that I was able to experience you here on earth & we will meet again. XOXOX

DIANE/MOM TO ANGEL JIMMY BROZZETTI ON DEC 7, 2007

Getting ready for Christmas in Heaven must be fun, Sprinkle some hugs & kisses down to us who miss all our angels

DIANE/MOM TO ANGEL JIMMY BROZZETTI ON DEC 11, 2007

Nick I light this candle for the world to see what a handsome angel you are, May your light shine bright God Bless."

MOMMY NICKY'S MOM ON DEC 23, 2007

I ask God everyday "why" I feel so abandoned. It's not your fault but WHY???? You were my LIFE, MY WORLD and MY FUTURE.

KIM BEELER. MATTHEW BEELER'S MOMMY ON DEC 23, 2007

Thinking of Nicky today. Such a handsome young man with a beautiful shining spirit. God Bless

MOMMY MERRY CHRISTMAS ON DEC 25, 2007

Nicky... Please watch over Mommy, I need your guidance. Help me find peace within... I love you... Merry Xmas... Love Mommy

MOMMY I. MISS YOU ON DEC 25, 2007
My wish is to find joy and life again... I wish to be happy again...

MOMMY 2. YEARS... ON DEC 29, 2007
I still can't beleive your gone, God knows how I miss u... I miss your hugs... I miss hearing your voice... xoxoxxo

GRAM #. 1. GRAM ON DEC 30, 2007
OH NICKY, MY DAYS & NIGHTS! YOU ARE ON MY MIND EVERY MINUTE OF THE DAY. MISS SEEING YOU ON LINE!! AMEN

DIANE/MOM TO ANGEL JIMMY BROZZETTI ON JAN 3, 2008
I light this candle for U Nick & UR family The Beginning of a New Year brings so much pain for us missing our angels

SHELLY ALWAYS KENNYS MOM ON JAN 3, 2008
THINKING OF YOU, HANDSOME NICK & SENDING MOM MUCH LOVE & STRENGTH. XXOO

ELLEN MUM OF ADAM GILMOUR ON JAN 3, 2008
Thinking of you and mom today Nick and sending big hugs to you both xxxx

MARGUERITE WARD MOM TO ANGEL BRANDI ON JAN 4, 2008
Thinking of your precious angel Nick today. Praying that God's love surrounds you and brings you comfort.

GEORGIE-HOLLY CLARKE MUM ON JAN 4, 2008
It's my honour 2 light this candle in memory of a brave young man. My daughter passed from this disease, i no your pain

PATRICIA/MOM TO JOHN ERMATINGER ON JAN 4, 2008
Thinking of u and lighting this candle. Sending prayers to all who love u. Fly high angel.

MOM OF JONATHAN BREWER ON JAN 8, 2008
Once an Angel on Earth & Now an Angel in Heaven. Love to all...

LISA PERFETTI ON JAN 9, 2008
Hi Nicky! Sending you and your Mom Hugs and Kisses. Keep watching over your Mom. We all miss you.

DIANE/MOM TO ANGEL JIMMY BROZZETTI ON JAN 11, 2008
"May your hearts be filled with beautiful memories of your sweet angel now and always."

LISA ANGEL MOM TO TRAVIS WOERNER 16 ON JAN 13, 2008
You will find that when all of your friends and family are gone, your angel families still care.

KIM BEELER. MATTHEW BEELER'S MOMMY ON JAN 14, 2008

Remembering precious Nick and sending hugs of support to your mom. You are not alone. We understand. xoxo

CAMILLE, MOM TO ANGE FRANCESCO LOCCISANO ON JAN 14, 2008

God Bless you Nick. I know you are lighting up heaven. Many blessings to you Michele***

LUANN (JOHNNA'S GRAMMA) ON JAN 15, 2008

God bless your broken heart Michele. Sending hugs of comfort to you... xoxoxo

LENE ANGEL MICHAEL DAVIES SIGLES MUM ON JAN 16, 2008

Thinking of you and your family beautiful Nick. RIP mate.

GRAM #1 BABSIE ON JAN 16, 2008

"Nicky, I miss U. everything is see IS you! Not a day goes by that u're not on my mind You are at peace. Love U

ELLEN MUM OF ADAM GILMOUR ON JAN 23, 2008

Nick thinking of you and mom... Help her to make decision... Hugs to you both xxxx

DIANNE/MOM OF ANGEL NICHOLAS WHITE ON JAN 24, 2008

May those who miss you dearly be always blessed by ur loving presence & continued guidance to lead them home

MOMMY TOTALLY DEVOTED ON FEB 4, 2008
I am so thankful for friends who truely realize what a lose of a child means... Luv Mommy

DIANE/MOM TO ANGEL JIMMY BROZZETTI ON FEB 11, 2008
Nick Happy Valentines Day sending lots of hugs n kisses! A special candle burns for you in ur loving memory RIP

CAMILLE, MOM 2. ANGEL FRANCESCO LOCCISANO ON FEB 12, 2008
Dear Nicky, God bless you in heaven. Please watch over your mom. I know you and my Frankie are friends in heaven. xoxox

JUDY OF CHARLES WILDHAGEN ON FEB 14, 2008
Happy Valentines Day sweetie, sending hugs to you in heaven and keeping you in my thoughts always

MOMMY PLEASE COME VISIT ME ON FEB 16, 2008
I wish I could see your smile and beautiful eyes...photos & videos are not real...I wish I could hold you again.

DIANNE/MOM OF ANGEL NICHOLAS WHITE ON FEB 17, 2008
May the glow of ur heavenly light shine down upon those whose hearts are shattered & comfort them w/everlasting love

LINDA MOM OF MICHAEL ARRIGO ON FEB 23, 2008

If ever there is a tomorrow when we're not together remember U are braver, stronger than U believe and I'm always with U.

JUDY ON MAR 5, 2008

God Bless and Keep You in His Loving Arms.

DIANE/MOM TO ANGEL JMMY BROZZETTI ON MAR 6, 2008

Many hearts R broken without you here. U R loved & missed by so many. Sending U a big hug!" RIP

JUDY OF CHARLES WILDHAGEN ON MAR 6, 2008

May peace fall softly upon your world and stay forever in your heart, love always xxx

JUDY OF CHARLES WILDHAGEN ON MAR 11, 2008

Remembering the days of long ago: thinking about the generations past... Love always

CAMILLE MOM OF ANGEL FRANCESCO LOCCISANO ON MAR 13, 2008

Thinking of you Nicky and my Frankie too. The pain never goes away. How do we live with out our sons... Love to Michele

PASSING BY ON MAR 17, 2008

What a remarkable young man. May the good lord watch over you on earth and your son above.

CAROL MOM MATTHEW MULLIS ON MAR 20, 2008

I light this candle Nicky in memory of you, The beauty of u'r heart will forever light the heavens.

MOMMY HAPPY EASTER MY LOVE ON MAR 22, 2008

Skina marinki dinki dink, skina marinki doo,... Mommy Loves You!

CAMILLE MOM OF ANGEL FRANCESCO LOCCIANO ON MAR 23, 2008

Thinking of you this Easter in heaven. Rest in peace with the angels and our Lord

DIANE/MOM TO ANGEL JIMMY BROZZETTI ON MAR 29, 2008

Good night sweet angel, let your loving family know you are near Have a wonderful night in heaven God Bless

MOMMY: YOU'RE MY EVERYTHING ON APR 3, 2008

Wherever did you go~I wait for you day & night to come home~I miss you more than anything in this world~ Luv, Mama

GRAM SKIPPER ON APR 3, 2008

Nicky, your on my mind every day, every breath I take I MISS YOU SO
!!! XXXOOOO

MOMMY: ˜I MISS YOU SO MUCH˜ ON APR 19, 2008

It's late Nicky, Mommy waits for you to come home˜I know you are with me˜but I miss your hugs˜ Luv, Mamma

---

DIANE/MOM TO ANGEL JIMMY BROZZETTI ON APR 29, 2008

I light this candle for U Handsome angel may UR light shine bright in the hearts of UR loved ones God Bless

---

GRAM #. 1. GRAM ON APR 29, 2008

My dearest Skipper, another month has gone by, the 29th once again, I lit a CANDLE for you this morning. xxxoo

---

MOMMY ˜WHERE ARE YOU˜ ON MAY 6, 2008

˜Life with you was like a dream I miss you terribly˜ Luv, Mommy

---

CAMILLE MOM OF ANGEL FRANCESCO LOCCISANO ON MAY 6, 2008

Nicky, stay close to your Mom this mothers day. I don't know how I will handle first Mother day without my Frankie.

GRAM BABSIE ON MAY 11, 2008

Skipper, I miss u my Blessed Grandson! I GO BACK IN TIME NICKY, everyday. I LOVE YOU SOOOOOOOOOOO

GRAM*#1 AKA BABSIE ON MAY 11, 2008

Nicky, me again! I read all the candles lit for U, There are so many Blessed folks..." Thank you everyone!

DIANE/MOM TO ANGEL JIMMY BROZZETTI ON MAY 20, 2008

Good night sweet angel you & your family are always in my thoughts & prayers God Bless

DIANE/MOM TO ANGEL JIMMY BROZZETTI ON MAY 25, 2008

Wishing U & UR family a Happy Memorial Day filled with beautiful memories of years past God Bless sweet angel RIP

DIANE/MOM TO ANGEL JIMMY BROZZETTI ON JUN 1, 2008

Hold on to your wonderful memories of your loved one..For they are always around us God Bless (HUGS)

CAMILLE MOM TO ANGEL FRANCESCO LOCCISANO ON JUN 19, 2008

Nicky, thinking of you on your Birthday and praying for your Mom. As mothers are hearts are broken 4ever.

JUDY ON JUN 20, 2008
Happy Birthday in Heaven Nick. God Bless You. Say a prayer for your Gram and Mom today. They miss you so much.

MOMMY HAPPY BIRTHDAY BABY ON JUN 21, 2008
I know you were with us on ur special 21st Bday ˜I fely you all around˜

DIANE/MOM TO ANGEL JIMMY BROZZETTI ON JUL 6, 2008
"Nick you are so loved and missed... Sending hugs to you and family... YOU will meet again xxx"

DIANE/MOM TO ANGEL JIMMY BROZZETTI ON JUL 13, 2008
"Saying hi to let U know I'm thinking of U today. Smile down on your love ones. Ur smile is sunshine (HUGS)"

MOMMY TIME GOES BY, ON JUL 20, 2008
Every minute that goes by I miss you so much... Mimmy xoxoxo

MY HEART IS EMPTY WITHOUT MY SON
LETTERS TO HEAVEN

THIS WORLD WAS GRACED WITH YOUR PRESENCE
MICHELE – MOTHER (JAN 2006)

MY SON'S LEGACY BEGAN THE MOMENT OF HIS CONCEPTION. AS I CARRIED him for nine beautiful months, I sang to Nicky each night and thanked God for his gift. Nicky never took life for granted, he was a simple soul who loved so graciously.

OUR BOND WAS UNCONDITIONALLY FROM THE MOMENT HE WAS BORN, AS THE nurse placed him upon my stomach on June 20th, 1987 Nicky looked dagger into my eyes. I knew at that moment he was a unique soul. He never left my hip until the very end on December 29th, 2005. For 18 years we were loyal to one another. Nicky gave me the meaning of life I have no right to expect nor will anyone ever take from me. Nicky was a charismatic soul, always worried about others. Never showed pity or concession for what God had in store for him.

Our lives were blessed to have known Nicky. We loved and adored him immensely. Everyone that was graced with his presence admired his love for life, his contagious smile, his wisdom, his hardy laugh, and most of all his patience. Nicky loved his sneakers, now I know why, because he knew, no one could walk in them.

He projected a strong sense of how life should be lived to those around him through his faith, love, and respect. Please, Can I, Thank you and I love you were a small part of his daily vocabulary. He always had the utmost respect for everyone he met, never greedy, needy, or disloyal. Nicky was a peaceful soul, he never entertained chaos in his life.

God called for him because of his purity. There are times I feel guilty that I brought Nicky into this cruel world, yet after I ponder those thoughts I comfort my broken heart and say, I am proud to have had a son that illuminated presence to those lives he touched.

Thank you Nicky for teaching me patience. my life has been slightly alleviated God is holding you in his arms and has welcomed you into heaven where we will all meet again one day.

[a]Mom, I love you, I'm going home were the last words he spoke between his tiny breaths before God took my son.

I love You Nicky, Mommy

OUR RELATIONSHIP TRANSCENDS DEATH

My Son, My Life, My Everything...

Photos, videos, songs & cherished loving memories are all I have left of you.

You & Me against the world, sometimes it felt like you and me against the world...and when one of us is gone...and one of us is left to carry on...then remembering alone will get us through...think about the days of me and you... You & Me against the world.

Nicky,

Mommy misses you so very much. I lived my life for you...and now... I am so empty inside wondering really [a]where you are[o] and if you need anything...a gentle hug and a kiss goodnight. I know you have come to me since you left on December 29th, 2005, but your physical being is so far away it is tearing my heart apart. I want to see you, feel your little heartbeat, hold your hand, and sing to you. I miss our slumber parties, our late night movies, listening to your dreams, taking pictures with our cell phones, and holding you in my arms all through the night, laying my head on your shoulder.

You filled my life with so much love, never judging,

never disrespectful, never asked for pity or concession. Always saying ªthank youº even throughout your pain. You were PERFECT. You always worried about everyone else because you were SELFLESS. I am blessed to have been chosen to guide you through your life here on earth, but now, you have been chosen to go home and live your life free of pain & suffering. I will do my best as each day & night goes by to remember our special talks and the messages you sent during the weeks before you died...

You said ªMom your new life will begin after 40, I promise you. I will try to stay strong by those words, but it will be very difficult as I sift through your beloved things you left behind.

My sadness will remain until you meet me at the end of that white tunnel you saw a few months ago when Mikey died, your brother from another mother. All of our cherished memories together will get me through each day know ing we both experienced a life together that was full of unconditional LOVE, HAPPINESS & our deep connection for one another.

Thank You Nicky for Loving Me So Very Much...

Love Mommy 1/24/2006

MY HEART ACHES EVERY DAY & NIGHT...WITHOUT YOU

2/6/2006

Without you, my heart aches...every minute of the day...and with each passing moment. Our moments together expressed a love that is unconditional...a love that transcends death...but I await that moment...the moment I am not afraid to see you again. Few may understand our deep connection... an unconditional love... when you can express yourself eternally and externally. our love transcends death Nicky...in your heart you knew where love was to transpire...within our faith. You have made an impact to so many, yet, one day, they will know where you came from...and realize... God exists...within you.

Lovingly, Mommy

HAPPY VALENTINE'S DAY MY SWEETHEART

2/14/2006

Nicky, my love, my son, my support... Today is our second holiday away from one another. Five years ago on this date 2/14, you endured your first painful surgery (the removal of your tumor on your fibula). As I walked to you in the recovery room, you yelled out, "Mommy, it hurts, did they get it all out?" My eyes filled with tears looking into your eyes and took a breath. At that moment I felt helpless, yet in the midst of what we were up against, God gave me the strength to take your hand and guide you through these last five years of your life with never-ending happiness, unconditional love, and precious days together. I never dreamed that my son would be taken so far away from me where I could not walk into your bedroom and watch you sleep, sing to you, hold you in my arms, listen to your loving ways you spoke to me, and the way you stood by me. Instead, the disease consumed our lives. I always thought I would see you playing basketball for your college, and then playing with your children. A sport you loved and looked forward to so much. My heart is suffering so much that it will never heal. My beautiful angel is gone from me forever. I will never hear your laugh again or see your beautiful smile. Months pass, I grieve quietly, crying alone. The dates on the calendar that were so important, are not anymore because I cannot share them with you. The daily routines are mundane so to speak, the pain is taking over. Everything reminds me of you and I cannot escape as the pain flows through my veins and sears my soul.

Oh God Nicky, where are you? I wait for you every day to come through that door. Somedays I just want to come see you but I know it would be wrong to do such a silly thing. No one will ever understand how I feel, you loved me with no judgment, no opinion, and no ego. You have completed me, Nicky, with your selfless trait towards everyone you came in contact with. A trait in which you instilled in many, and for this, I thank you because you have made an impact on so many...

THANK YOU, GOD, FOR THE GIFT OF MY SON, NICK

TWO MONTHS HAVE PASSED

March 1st, 2006

I will never understand...how you came into my life and left me with the limitless devotion & love you so freely exemplified.

I will never understand why you would always stand by me all these years without judgment.

I will never understand when people were cruel, you would overlook their "ignorance."

I will never understand where your patience and strength came from.

You sheltered me through the harshness of life with your words of wisdom even as a child.

When you wrote on your website (myspace.com) last year, "you will never be on my level" others would take a cue from your inspiring words.

You and I both are old souls, we have been here many times. You came here to teach many lessons. Perhaps for a few, it may take quite a number of visits, eventually, it may kick in. You're no longer on an earth plane where we look upon one another with animosity, jealousy, judgment, or even hatred. You have graduated and now in a place that is truly loving & free of pain. You tried your hardest to be the peacemaker, but more importantly, your antics displayed a soul of a true man with an honest heart.

It gives me comfort knowing I experienced this wonderful love from someone who loved so selflessly, my son.

My song I sang to you from when you were born as I rocked you to sleep at night until the night you left us,

LaLaLaLaLaLaLaLaLaLaLaLa, Nicky is a special angel above...Nicky is a little angel loved and cared by all, LaLa,La,La,La,La,La,La,La,La

xoxoxoxoxox Mommy

MY NICKY,

March 25th, 2006

Mommy misses you so very much. From the moment I wake until I close my eyes, I know our connection is within our souls no matter where you are. As I grieve for you each day, I am getting through it. The daily visits & connections with you are overwhelming to mommy, yet knowing your safe in ways I never thought possible. The heavy blanket is lifting slowly. My heart knows where you are is safe. You are alive more than ever, working for me in heaven watching over Mommy.

Our soul connection will remain as I feel you, as I see you, and most importantly as I hear you every day, all day long talking to Mommy. In my dream last night, [a]I'm so sorry Mommy, I wish things were different, my life may have been short but it was enriched by your unconditional love.

Until we meet again, Mommy

UNCONDITIONAL LOVE MOTHER AND SON

April 2, 2006

Often words go unspoken, yet our words were never unspoken, we always spoke the truth. The truth without judging, the truth through respect for one another. A teenager/child who held no grudges and would never betray his friends, loyal and true blue was this gift only given to you. This is the uncommon bond that you and I shared, a bond in which no one will ever take from meIt is still quite difficult to get used to this new way of life, it will never be the same without you. Holidays are upon us and I am numb, strangers talk to me and I do not even hear what they are saying, I don't care what they have to say. By its very nature, life is a potpourri of events that are filtered through our emotional, physical, mental, and spiritual selves. The purpose of life is to learn to appreciate these various aspects of ourselves just you did with your experience through life's ups and downs which made you grow in the knowledge and wisdom of yourself as the loving and spiritual being you exemplified. You accomplished this in a very short, yet quite a "complete" life. The love we shared since your birth was strong enough to move the earth. You're by my side whether awake or asleep, now rest your journey is through— everlasting life has been given to you.

I LOVE YOU UNCONDITIONALLY, MOMMY

A CHILD ON LOAN

Michele Mother April 8th, 2006

My Nicky... I am so proud of you, so proud that I was your mommy. Your soul was created to enhance the lives of strangers who became a friend, yet they were drawn to you because of the depth of your soul. What a gift!

"A CHILD ON LOAN"

My child was born into this life. How proud I was to have a son sent from above. Not knowing the future, days flew by. Watching you grow, seeing you cry. Soley guiding you as best I could, knowing YOU understood. Why you were placed on this earth on loan. The many challenges you faced will never be erased. Carved like a stone in my mind memories of unconditional love left behind. A tortured mind you did possess, you just could never get any rest. Need for you to go on, so you choose the great beyond. Tears are shed by all you knew but I know that we must always be GRATEFUL for the love we knew, from the child God loaned to ME.

ALL MY LOVE, MOMMY

YOU SET THE TONE

June 1, 2006

NICKY... I MISS YOU SO SO MUCH... EIGHTEEN YEARS OLD... A MAN... A REAL MAN...who never held a grudge...you made everyone laugh with you're quirky sense of humor. no one will EVER fill ur shoes...young and old...you had it all together at eighteen years old! wow, it's amazing the impact you made on so many...lessons that you taught...even though your high school would not allow you to walk on stage with all your friends who stood by you, you graduated into a life only suitable for you...u graduated from this life with class and style, a few traits you carried some will never "get"... I am so fortunate & blessed... I love you my baby, MOMMY

TO MY CHILD

June 9th, 2006

I always smiled when I saw your face and laughed when I felt like crying. I always let you choose your clothing and smiled just because. I always stepped over my laundry to pick you up and take you to the park. I always left the dishes in the sink and watched you put your puzzles together as you taught me precious moments of quality, loving time together°. We would blow bubbles in the backyard/porch and I would never yell or grumble when you would scream for the ice cream truck when he came by. I never ᵃworriedº about where you were going or who you were going with or second guess your decisions. I would always let you roll my rum balls and help me back Christmas cookies for all our friends and family and never tried to fix them. You would have not one but two Happy Meals from Mc Donalds so you could have both toys. I would always hold you in my arms and tell you stories when you were born and how much your life meant to me. You would always splash in the tub, making a mess and I would never get angry. I would snuggle with you for hours as we watched TV/Movies as I ran my fingers through your beautiful hair and thank God that He has given me the greatest gift ever as I kissed you goodnight, and gave you a squeeze, tighter and tighter, it is then I thanked God for you, and ask Him for nothing, except for ONE MORE DAY. There are no more days now that you are gone, loneliness creeps within as I wake up and go to sleep. Memories will NEVER prevail over the pain inside of mommy, no one will ever understand a lost child.

Mommy

HE ONLY TOOK MY HAND

August 7th, 2006

Last night while I was trying to sleep, My son's voice I did hear I opened my eyes and looked around But he did not appear.

He said "Mom you've got to listen, You've got to understand God didn't take me from you, Mom He only took my hand When I called out in pain that night, The instant that I died,

He reached down and took my hand, And pulled me to his side. He pulled me up and saved me From the misery and pain

My body was hurt so badly inside, I could never be the same. My search is really over now, I've found happiness within.

All the answers to my empty dreams And all that might have been.

I love you and miss you so, And I'll always be nearby. My body's gone forever, But my spirit will never die!

And so, you must go on now, Live one day at a time. Just understand-

God did not take me from you, He only took my hand. MOMMY

HAPPY HALLOWEEN YOUR FAVORITE HOLIDAY

October 31, 2006

HAPPY HALLOWEEN MY NICKY POO. THIS WEEKEND IS MOST DIFFICULT FOR ME. HALLOWEEN WAS YOUR FAVORITE HOLIDAY BECAUSE YOU WERE THE BIGGEST PROFESSIONAL PRANKSTER. I REMEMBER ONE YEAR WHEN I DRESSED YOU AND SISSY UP. SHE WAS WEDNESDAY FROM THE ADAMS FAMILY AND YOU WERE JACKIE "O". AND WHEN MOMMY TOOK YOU TO SALEM MASSACHUSETTES AND SISSY WAS SO CUTE, SHE WORE THE PINK FELT SKIRT W/ THE POODLE ON IT FROM THE 50'S. AND YOU WERE A PUMPKIN. OH AND LET'S NOT FORGET YOUR SPIDERMAN COSTUME FROM NYU. YOUR LONG SLENDER LEGS OH HOW FUNNY YOU WERE, IT WAS SO DAM TIGHT AND HOW U WERE PROUD OF THAT BODY, NOT TO MENTION YOUR PACKAGE! LOL.

WHEN YOU WERE 11 I TOOK YOU TO THE REAL AMITYVILLE HOUSE ON HALLOWEEN, AND YOU BOTH WALKED UP TO THE DOOR FOR "TREATS". AS YOU WALKED BACK TO ME I TOOK A PHOTO OF YOU & WHEN I DEVELOPED IT, THERE WAS A WHITE LIGHT ALL AROUND YOUR LITTLE BODY.

BUT AS YOU GOT OLDER YOU LOVED TO PLAN YOUR HALLOWEEN WITH YOUR FRIENDS, EGGING, THE TOILET PAPER, SHAVING CREAM...ONE YEAR THE COPS WERE CHASING YOU AND YOU JUMPED OVER A FENCE AND SCRAPPED UR LEG VERY BADLY, BUT YOU NEVER GOT CAUGHT! THAT'S MY BOY˜! "MR. SMOOTHY" I CAN'T IMAGINE WHAT YOU WOULD HAVE DONE THIS YEAR IF YOU WERE HERE, YOU ALWAYS HAD THE PLAN TO DO SOME CRAZY SHIT. DON'T YOU WORRY, MOMMY WILL MAKE UP FOR YOU. I KNOW YOU'RE GOING TO EXPERIENCE A WONDERFUL HALLOWEEN WITH MIKEY, CARL, GUERMO & STEVEN. YOUR NOT ALONE MY BABY. LUV U MORE THAN LIFE ITSELF, MOMMY

HAPPY THANKSGIVING BABE

NOVEMBER 22ND, 2006

HAPPY THANKSGIVING MY DARLING... LAST YEAR AT THIS TIME I WAS PREPARING FOR YOUR THANKSGIVING DINNER. NEVER DREAMING IT WOULD BE OUR LAST THANKSGIVING TOGETHER. ALTHOUGH YOU WERE IN THE HOSPITAL.

MOMMY MADE EVERY EFFORT TO MAKE SURE YOU CAME HOME FOR THE AFTERNOON. DR. RAUSEN ALLOWED YOU TO COME HOME FOR 6 HOURS VIA AMBULANCE. YOUR WALKING ABILITY WAS COMING TO AN END BUT YOU WERE STILL DETERMINED TO FIGHT NO MATTER WHAT. AS YOU SAT IN YOUR WHEELCHAIR IN FRONT OF THE TINY TABLE IN THE LIVING ROOM, YOU ASKED MOMMY TO BRING OUT THE TURKEY SO YOU COULD LOOK AT IT. AS YOU STARED AT THE TURKEY, TEARS STREAMED FROM YOUR EYES. AS I WATCHED YOUR EMOTION I FELT HELPLESS BUT

I COULD NOT LET YOU SEE MY PAIN. GRAMMA MADE YOUR FAVORITE MASHED POTATOES. BUT YOUR APPETITE WAS NOT THE GREATEST, YOU WERE VERY WEAK. CARESS CAME BY TO SPEND SOME TIME WITH YOU. TODAY I WENT BACK TO OUR OLD APARTMENT TO SEE YOUR ROOM. THE PERSON WHO LIVES THERE WAS NICE ENOUGH TO LET ME IN. I CRIED A LITTLE BUT IT WAS NOT THE SAME, I KNEW YOU WERE NOT THERE BUT SUBCONSCIOUSLY I WAS LOOKING FOR YOU.

MOMMY IS SO GRATEFUL FOR HAVING YOU IN MY LIFE. YOU WERE INSPIRING AND CREATED A LEGACY THAT WILL LIVE FLOAT THROUGH ETERNITY. I SIT HERE IN AWE OF YOUR SPIRIT AND UNSELFISHNESS. I HAVE NOT MET ANYONE YET THAT HAS ONLY A SMALL PERCENTAGE OF YOUR CHARACTER. YOU ALWAYS HAD THE UTMOST RESPECT. I MISS YOU SO MUCH NICKY BECAUSE YOU WOULD NEVER LEAVE MOMMY ALONE ON A HOLIDAY. I WAS GOING TO TAKE UP GRAMMAS INVITE FOR TURKEY DINNER BUT IT IS A TENDER AND EMOTIONAL DAY FOR OUR FAMILY AND I CHOOSE TO BE WHERE I WAS LAST YEAR WITH YOU. OUR FAMILY WILL NEVER BE THE SAME WITHOUT YOU.

LOVINGLY, MOMMY

MERRY CHRISTMAS MY SON, 1ST XMAS WITHOUT YOU

DECEMBER 25TH, 2006

Your presence is sadly missed everyday-memories of you and your beautiful heart & smile swirl through my head-night and day.

I know you are at peace & pain-free my love, yet the emptiness will never ever dissipate-You have blessed our family with a beautiful gift this holiday, thank you, Nicky. Last year when you opened my Xmas gift to you, you just starred at it as your eyes filled with tears. As I read your card that Jackie helped you write because you couldn't see or write very well, I cried inside as I read it, you always wrote from your heart with so much appreciation.

Life is so strange Nick, you have taught me so much these last 18 years. Your humbleness and patience were EXTRAORDINAIRE. Christmas will never be the same without you-I hold so many dear memories in my heart but I miss you now more than EVER.

LOVINGLY, MOMMY

JULY 2007

Nicky's legacy continues as our family was blessed with a baby boy one year to the month of Nicky's passing. Little Angelo is quite amazing, his smile is contagious, his laugh is HARDY...he just laughs and smiles all day long. I am in total amazement when I see my grandson, he just stares at me, and when I hold him to sleep he just stares and is so content. I sing him to him and he just stares at me. Grateful for this wonderful blessing.

TIMELINE
1987

BORN IN NEW YORK ON JUNE 20, 1987.

THE WORSE DAY OF OUR LIVES (NOVEMBER 9TH, 2001)

Michele - Mother

I NEVER IMAGINED HOW DIFFICULT IS WOULD BE TO RAISE A CHILD ALONE especially a child with cancer. (Ewings Sarcoma)

IT ALL STARTED AT A BASKETBALL GAME IN 2001 IN TUCKAHOE, NY. HE WAS injured by another player who kicked him in the leg while Nicky was dribbling the ball. He tragically fell on the court holding his leg. I jumped off the benches and ran to my son, no one, not even the coach came to see if Nicky was ok, they all just kept playing the game around me as I tried to help my son off the court.

A few months after this injury and while visiting his father for the summer grew a large bump on his lower leg under his knee, exactly where he was injured. Got the call from his Dad a few weeks before high school started, I immediately brought him back downstate took him to the doctor, and was referred to the top specialist immediately. We scheduled surgery on 11/9/2001. On that Friday morning, my mother, Nicky, and I drove down to Beth Israel for his biopsy. He was so strong and smiled at me as he went into the surgery room. After 4 hours, Dr.Kenan came down to tell us the worst news of my life. Nicky had cancer and needs to see an Oncologist on Monday. I was devastated and was in shock. I went to the recovery room and saw Nicky; I could hear him from afar, Mommy, Mommy. I walked over to him and looked at him with tears starting in my eyes. He said, "Mommy did they get it all out?" I took a deep breath and said we have to use special medicine to make your bump shrink. I then started to tell him how handsome he looked and we will be going home shortly.

CHEMO STARTS IMMEDIATELY (2001-2003)

Nicky started his chemo immediately; his treatment was to last one year. Instead, it has lasted almost four years. He has lost out on school, playing sports, dating girls, and graduating this year with his friends.

After losing all I ever worked for I had to rely on Social Services and Eastchester Housing Assistance. The trips to the hospital were very expensive. I had no income, just a small unemployment check.

After one year of Nicky receiving the "red devil" cocktail, his hair was growing back and Nicky was gaining weight. He was looking so dapper! We went for our monthly visits including the CAT scan on his lungs which was due.

The results came back, Nicky had a relapse, and we had to start chemo again. Nicky needed lung surgery on his right lung to remove as many tumors as they could. His surgery lasted five hours. We once again had to start treatment just after three months of a normal life. Since this, Nicky has undergone another lung surgery because the tumors were traveling to the other lung.

GONG TO LOURDES FOR A MIRACLE (MAY 2005)

Nicky went to Lourdes France for the first time with his gramma in 2004. I was unable to go because I was not financially able to do so. So the following year a special person with whom I met at a fundraiser a few years ago has raised enough funds so that Nicky and I both can go to Lourdes together in May 2005. We are very grateful for this blessing and the blessing of having people who really care to help us with this wish.

I heard people take their loved ones to this special place called Lourdes, France to receive blessings and miracles happen. Thousands of sick people travel there every year for hope, miracles, and healing. Nicky was unable to attend school and was Catholic, the bishop of Lourdes approved for my son to receive his Confirmation. He chose the name, Anthony.

THE WORSE DAY OF MY LIFE, I LOST MY SON DECEMBER 29TH, 2005

Nicky's wish was to be home for the holidays, he loved being home in his own bed. Father Raasner came by on December 27th early in the morning to give Nicky communion and also his last rites. That night prior to his passing Nicky and I watched "The Forty-Year-Old Virgin." He LOVED funny movies. I slept with my son every night next to him on an air mattress on the floor, but that night when all the lights were out, my son asked me to crawl into bed with him. It was a twin bed. Nicky lost his feeling from his hips into his legs two months prior because the tumors spread down into his spine and later lost part of his vision & hearing because the tumors went onto his skull pressing on his brain. So that night (Dec. 27th) was a special night, we talked, laughed, took pictures with his camera of us, and cuddled. I wrapped myself around him and never let him go until we woke up the next morning. I told Nicky that we would be going on a lot of trips after the New Year, he said to me "Mom next year is going to be a better year for you Mom" when he did not include himself in that sentence, I knew what he was telling me.

My routine every day was to bathe him from head to toe. His skin was so dry I had to put moisturizer all over him two to three times a day. His favorite was the cucumber moisturizer. We went down to the clinic for a blood transfusion even though it was not needed, Nicky had hope still he was going to fight his cancer. When we left the clinic, as we drove in the ambulance back home, he stopped breathing. I was hysterical and we went to the closest hospital for oxygen. Once he got his oxygen, Nicky said "Mom calm down everything is going to be ok." We then proceeded to go back home with only two tanks of oxygen to get him home. The tanks were small and could only last fifty more minutes. We arrived at home to find out we have no more oxygen, the paramedics had to take the tanks back. I was again hysterical. I went into the bedroom to tell Nicky we have no more oxygen and we need to go back to the hospital until the morning so that Hospice could set up a tank in his room.

He did not want to go, he said "Mom, I am going to be okay." I left his room not knowing whether to call the paramedics, so a family friend took charge and called 911. They came in five minutes. We went back to a local hospital for just the night (Dec.28th) and came back home that afternoon (Dec. 29th) around 3 pm. During the night I watched his breaths grow shorter and shorter. I was not ready to let my Nicky go. Hospice came over and directed us to give him morphine to alleviate his pain and eventually alleviate his fight for life. I sang to Nicky a song when he would go to sleep a night and again the night he was passing, "You and Me Against The World" by Helen Reddy. He was so peaceful, he would look at me and smile. At 8:30 pm, I was alone in the room with my son. I whispered in his ear what I was told by hospice to say because my son was so worried about me, he could not let go until he knew I was going to be ok. I said, "Nicky, Mommy loves you so very much and I am going to miss you like no other, you were a gift to me and I am going to be okay, please do not worry about Mommy, I will be strong for you." I raised my hands to God and asked God to please take my son in his loving arms, free him from his pain. Thank you, God, for blessing me with a wonderful son.

I then kissed him and said in his little ear, Nicky please watch over Mommy,

I love you, my baby. As I pulled away, his eyes opened looking right at me intensely. At that moment, I felt a powerful force hit me through my stomach and collapsed to the floor, a family friend carried me onto the porch ad wrapped me in a blanket. ten minutes later I was called to go back into his room, I was scared, the lights were on and his oxygen mask was off his face. I started screaming hysterical "PUT HIS OXYGEN ON NOW" MY SON MY SON, NICKY, they were trying to calm me but I could not stop crying and screaming. He looked so peaceful his hands were across his tummy and his eyes were closed forever. I started to put moisturizer all over him, I laid with him and just held him so tightly.

The news traveled so quickly. All his friends were lined up outside with candles and flowers. I invited them in to say goodbye to their best friend. I could not beleive how many kids came by. The look in their eyes were of so much pain. I am grateful that my son was blessed with so many beautiful friends.

P.S.

Nicky received communion everyday while at the hospital and at home, he had a shrine of Saints in a private space in his closet. During his quiet time he prayed faithfully.

TESTIMONIALS

HARD TO SAY GOODBYE

MY LOVING GRANDSON AKA ''SKIPPER' WAS MY LIFE. IN HIS EARLY YRS

HE COUL NOT WAIT TO RUN UP STAIRS TO ME... WHAT A WONDER- FUL ...GIFT HE GAVE ME ... HE LOVED TO DRAW THE ''TURTLES "" AT THE KITCHEN TABLE [WITH THE FATHER]. I REMENBER THE TIMES HE WOULD SAY 'OUR PRAYERS TOGETHER...WHEN I WAS BABYSITTING THE CHILDREN... ALSO, HE LOVED EVEN LITTLE 'GRASS HOPPERS' I WOULD PUT THEM IN A JAR. AND HE WOULD ALWAYS SAY ""''GRAM, LET THEM OUT ""'' OF THE JAR... ALSO LIGHTING BUGS..HE WOULD LET CAUGHT THEM OK MUCH LOVE GRAM

BARBARA FEYL

GRANDMOTHER January - 19 - 2006

THERES NOT A NIGHT THAT GOES BY THAT I DONT CRY MYSELF TO SLEEP. THE thought of saying goodbye to my friend, breaks my heart into a million pieces. Actually, i Never formally said go0dbye, but everytime i vistited nick, i always made sure i told him i loved him before i left. The last time i saw nick was 1 week before he passed. I was supposed to go visit him the night of the 29th, but before i left my house, Vito called me with the news. The feeling that came over me was undescribable. My knees gave out, and i fell on the floor i thought i was going to pass out. Deep down, i knew his day was coming, but nothing in this world could have prepared me for it. Nick was such a Wonderful AMAZING person. Knowing that he will not be around anymore makes me sick. There are so many things that remind me of him. Certain songs, sneakers, jokes, cars, and the thought of summer just makes me think of "Nick". It was so hard to believe that he was sick. He was so ill, yet never seemed it. He was so full of life, and i think thats why i was always in such denial. i thought he'd be around just as long as the rest of us..long enough to finish growing up together, to make memories, to go on vacations, to have kids, and to stay friends forever...until we all got old, and died together. But in nicks case, he wanted to lead the way. He went first, because we all know he was so brave.

I wish there was something i could have said or done, to take his pain away. i wish i could have just put him at ease. I know that all of our support corforted him, but i wish it was more than that.

Everday i wonder where he is, and what hes doing...i wonder if he's with mikey...i wonder if he is watching us, and playing jokes on us, or making fun of us. i wonder if he hears me when i talk to him...i wonder if he misses me...i could sit here and write forever...but i wont. Nickk, i love you & I miss you.

You were such a good friend. Watch over me. x0x
—Danielle Repetti

I HAVE BEEN BLESSED TO HAVE KNOWN YOU FOR 12 YEARS. IN THOSE YEARS you have taught me so much. You were my teacher. You gave me courage and you made me believe in the after life, when before there were doughts. You suffered so much for so long and never complained or gave up.always worrying about others. you were an extroadinery person. There is not a day that goes by that I don't think of you. I miss you very much. I thank you for being in my life and being my teacher. And sending me new friends. I will never forget our talks we had. And our special dinners they will always stay in my heart. save me a seat at that dinner table. Until we meet again.

Love and miss you always,
Ann Marie DeCairano January 19, 2006

NICKY, NOT A DAY GOES BY I DON'T MISS YOU, I FEEL YOU ALL AROUND ME. You were our gift and we will treasure the time spent with you forever. I am so thankful to you for all you have taught me. you have taught me how to share my feelings with others and about strength and courage. you were and are the best of the best and you will remain in my heart forever, we are never alone because as my heart beats i feel feel you . i love and miss you more with each passing day...until we meet again...

love you sweetie. jackie
dear friend January - 20 - 2006

MY RELATIONSHIP WITH NICKY WAS SHORT LIVED AND RELATIVELY NEW. WE first met at a casino night fund raiser and I was instantly interested in wanting to help him and getting to know him better. There was some thing special about this young man. I asked him what I could do for him, and his response was "Pray for me". I assured him that I would, but I insisted in knowing what he wanted (or needed) to help him during this difficult time in his life. He told me that he would love to go back to Lourdes...that there was a pilgrimage scheduled to leave on May 13th...that he had been there once before and yearned to go back. His faith and his belief in God struck me as unbelievable. How could someone so young (17 years of age) have such faith??? His spirituality was infectious. I promised him that night that he would be on that pilgrimage...and he was. With the help of our local Knights Of Columbus and a large private donation, Nicky and his mother went to Lourdes in May, 2005. Although Nicky did not receive the miracle we were all praying for, he did return from the trip somehow changed. We may never know how he was touched by the Spirit, but he was, and even his oncologist attested to this when he delivered a eulogy at the wake.

My relationship with Nicky was special to me...he touched my heart deeply and taught me about life and death. He carried his cross without question and carried it with a smile. He was an insiration to all who crossed his path and it was an honor to be a part of his life. I will miss his beautiful smile...but I know that Nicky is with our Creator...in a beautiful and perfect place called Heaven...no longer in pain...no longer suffering. Now I pray to Nicky to help all those left here on earth to cope with this tremendous loss...and I know he will do every thing he can because Nicky believed in living life to the fullest, which he did every day...and he wouldn't want us to live any other way.

Cheri

A new friend January - 20 - 2006

I THINK OF NICKY OFTEN. I REMEMBER THE FUNNY RESPECTFUL YOUNG MAN that would never leave my home without saying good-bye. Now, it breaks my heart that I had to say good-bye to him one last time. I am so sad not to see his face, and to know he is doing "o.k." I am overjoyed he is at peace with God. But, I wish you were here with us. Nicky has left something different, but special in everyones heart. That is why he is superior. His strenght, his love, and his joy of living will remain alive in all of us. We love you Nicky. Rest in Peace. Love you, Kathy and the boys.

Kathy O'Donnell

Friend to a superior young man January - 20 - 2006

NICKY, YOU WERE THE STRONGEST PERSON I HAVE EVER KNOWN. I MISS YOU IN a way i cant describe in words. Although i wish you were here with us, i find comfort in knowing you are no longer in pain, and you are in a much better place. You were one of a kind, your humor, your kindness, your courage, everything about you. I am so blessed to have been a part of your extraordinary life, and i thank you for being such a good friend to me. I guess i never wanted to know how sick you really were. Looking at you and being around you, your spirits were always so high, and from the outside it looked like there was nothing wrong.

The news was devastating and i didnt want to believe it. I never thought the day would really come and you would no longer be here. But you never really left. Your spirit is with all of us and you will live on in our hearts.

I wish i could see you again, spend a day with you, joke, laugh, hug you and tell you I Love You. But i tell you everyday and i know you hear me. We all know your looking down upon us smiling, still playing jokes and making all the angels laugh.

Dominique<3 dom
Close Friend January - 21 - 2006
You are truely an angel now

A CONTINUED UPDATE ON MY NICKY, HE WAS MY PRIDE AND JOY. HE WAS SO GREATFUL WHEN I WOULD PICK HIM UP AT SCHOOL TO TAKE HIM ICE SKATING. THEN HE LOVED TO WATCH THE HOCKEY PLAYERS. THEN IT WAS CHINESE FOOD... HE LOVED TO DRAW. HE WAS VERY CREATIVE... BUT MOST OF ALL HE LOVED HIS FAITH.

barbara feyl grandmother
January - 23 - 2006

IT WAS A GREAT PRIVILEGE TO BE ON PILGRIMAGE TO LOURDES WITH NICKY, his mother Michele and grandmother Barbara in May of 2005. Nicky said he found great peace in Lourdes— "can you help my mother?," he asked. He was thinking of her and we pray she has his peace now.

While in Lourdes, Nicky and his mom requested the Sacrament of Confirmation. The Bishop was called with this most special request and Nicky was Confirmed at the Cachot, the humble home of Bernadette Soubirious. It was from there that Bernadette went to the Grotto to meet the Mother of God and was promised happiness, not in this life, but in the other. Surely, the same will be true for Nicky. From the Cachot to the Grotto to Happiness! We wish peace and happiness to Nicky, his mom and each member of his family. Godspeed Nicky!

Marlene Watkins
Friend and Admirer January - 24 - 2006
Our Relationship Transends Death

MY SON, MY LIFE, MY EVERYTHING...PHOTOS, VIDEOS, SONGS & CHERISHED loving memories are all I have left of you. "You & Me against the world, sometimes it felt like you and me against the world...and when one of us is gone...and one of us is left to carry on...then remembering alone will get us through...think about the days of me and you...You & Me against the world"

Nicky, Mommy misses you so very much. I lived my life for you...and now... I am so empty inside wondering really "where you are" and if you need any- thing...a gentle hug and a kiss goodnight. I know you have come to me 6 times since you left on December 29th, 2005, but your physical being is so far away it is tearing my heart apart. I want to see you, feel your little heartbeat, hold your hand and sing to you. I miss our slumber parties, our late night movies, listening to your dreams, taking pictures with our cell phones, and holding you in my arms all through the night, laying my head on your shoulder.

You filled my life with so much love, never judging, never disrespectful, never asked for pity or concession.

Always saying "thank you" even throughout your pain. You were PERFECT. You always worried about everyone else because you were SELFLESS. I am blessed to have been chosen by God to guide you through your life here on earth, but now, you have been chosen by God to go home and live your life free of pain & suffering. I will do my best as each day & night goes by to remember our special talks and the messages you you sent during our talks. You said to me "Mom your new life will begin after 40, I promise you." I will try to stay strong by those words, but it will be very difficult as I sift through your beloved things you left behind.

My sadness will remain until you meet me at the end of the white tunnel. All of my cherished memories together will get me through each day knowing we both experienced a life together that was full of unconditional LOVE, HAPPINESS & our deep connection for one another.

Thank You Nicky for Loving Me So Very Much...

Love Mommy January - 24 - 2006

HI NICKY. I MISS YOU SO MUCH. I HAVE NO WORDS BECAUSE I WISH SO BADLY I can just say them to you. i realized that everything happens for a reason. i wake up everyday and you are the first person that i think about. mommy gave me your gold cross chain and i havent taken it off since. i wear the dogtag with your picture on it along with 1000 other people. you were loved so much and i think you already know that. i think everyday of how things could have been. me and you going on vacations and having little nieces and nephews. you have taught me so many lessons in life. you never realize what you have until its gone. you are my angel. you always have been and always will be. in a way, i feel more at peace now that your gone because i know that you are not suffering nomore. nomore pain no more needles nomore nurses and doctors in your face telling you what to do. and when i feel like i have noone some- times, i think of you and realize now i ALWAYS have someone. i know when you are with me and i kno when you are not. i hope when i do grow up and get married and have children, that my husband is just like you. you and daddy were the only men ive ever loved and the only people ive ever trusted. rest in peace sweetheart. i love you so much..no regrets and no goodbyes. ill see you soon.

- your little princess bianca sister
January - 25 - 2006Nicky,

MY HEART IS SO SAD, IT'S BEEN SAD SINCE YOU LEFT A MONTH AGO. I WISH I had one more chance to tell you what a special person you were and will continue to be in my life, I wish I had another chance to tell you I love you, to say one more hello, one more "see you later", one more hug.......I miss you sooooooo much...........

Yolanda
January - 29 - 2006

HEY ITS ME AGAIN JUST DROPPING BY BECAUSE I WAS THINKING ABOUT YOU. I miss you jellybean. i cant wait to see you. good things come to those who wait. xoxo i love you .

love bianca
sister January - 27 - 2006

NICKY IT HAS BEEN FIOUR WEEKS SINCE YOU LEFT US. I STILL CAN'T BELIEVE you are not here, i miss your face, your smile, your sense of humor., our talks.i miss you!!!
love you sweetie, jackie xoxoxoxo January - 27 - 2006 Alyce Davis-Lourdes pilgrim June 2004

I HAVE OFTEN THOUGHT ABOUT YOU, PRAYED FOR YOU SINCE MEETING YOU and Barb, your grandmother, on the pilgrimage to Lourdes in June 2004. I know your illness and suffering found a way into all of our hearts. I was moved by your sense of peace and acceptance about what was happening in your life. Being a nurse, working with cancer patients I had some understanding of what you had been through and what was to come in the course of your illness and treatment. I felt as a mother that need to nurture and protect, which you didn't need. You were too engaged with living and hanging on to hope and making the most of each day. I think of Barb and her overwhelming love and sorrow for you, so much so, that she brought you there to Lourdes, a witness to her faith and belief in the only things which really matter in life. She knew, you knew, and in your being there we all knew a little better about life and suffering and faith and acceptance. I will remember your life and death, my mother's birthday is December 29th, I am glad to have met you and witnessed the beautiful person that you are.

Alyce Davis
friend/fellow pilgrim January - 26 - 2006

———

As I THINK OF THE WONDERFUL YOUNG MAN THE SKIPPER WAS.

I only know that the Angels Greeted him as he enteredParadise.- Knowing the Smiles and Love Nicky shared, no word can explain.He was close to all whom he had contact with, a Love and Peace he had (with in) to share with every- one.The Skipper was an example to every-one,as he suffered in silence.

May everyone who knew him, remember how he loved to make all feel wel- come.I didn't know the Skipper for a long time ..I am only happy I had the opportunity to know him for the short time I did.He was the kind of Young Man, everyone would have liked to known.Peace to all you have touched in your special way.

Alyce Davis
friend/fellow pilgrim January - 26 - 2006

———

NICKY... ONE MONTH AND HERE'S ANOTHER MORNING WITHOUT YOU.

Here's another day; will I get through it without breaking down?

Haven't seen the sun since you've been gone. Like my heart, I lost it when you left me.

And it can't be found. How can I go on?

Nicky, I been living on memories of you and me.

All the love we shared. They're all here inside. Nicky, can you stop the rain from falling?

Won't you chase my clouds away?

I'd give anything to see your face again. Only you can stop these tears from falling

I can't face another day. Everywhere I go, I feel you there Following my footsteps like a shadow

Of my broken heart

Sometimes, it's a pair of passing eyes Or it's just the way someone is talking And there you are. Am I all alone?

Don't you ever look down and reach for me where we used to be? Is there any chance?

I just can't believe you're not here with me just me and you. How can I live without you, Nicky?

How could I have let you go? I am so alone...,

Mommy Misses You More Than Ever...

January 29th, 2006

NICKY B.

You were like a brother to me

I was hoping to God that you wouldn't leave I even said I wish I had your illness

So that you wouldn't be alone to face this I miss the late night talks I miss the crazy sleepwalks

I miss the laughter and crazy jokes

I miss the "suckas" and "ah-ha-ha's" like you don't even know There isn't one thing I wouldn't do to have you back here

But I promise I will be up there with you in coming years Sometimes I wondered why he challenged you

Someone so pure, happy, and full of youth

There are many more words that I'm missing that just can't explain The Loving, caring warrior that you became

I know that you are up there now

Looking down upon me, reassuring me it will all be okay somehow I now know why he took you away from us

It was to let us know that your job here was done

Because you influenced everyone one around you in ways that are possible to none

The truth is you have affected many like me and greater The proof all belies here in this paper

You were an angel on earth that had to be heard

God chose this path to show everyone around you, you were And boy does it hurt

But how come so early, why now

Why did we have to be stripped of you so soon

Why couldn't it have waited just a little so you, would've known just how many people loved you

Why couldn't it have waited, is it because God's greedy Or is it because you were just needed The truth Is all these why's won't answer a thing

But I think what's left of you in me will eventually answer everything Your aura just shined right through

Envy we did, since you did it with ease, the way none of us could do I just wanted to let you know we will be together again

You are sincerely missed, but the missing will end when we meet in heaven.

-Christian DeLaRosa Brother January - 29 - 2006

NICKY,

Its been a month now since I have heard your voice. I havent been able to sleep ever since. Your all I think about. I miss how when you were a little boy and you had a bad dream and you called for me to protect you, I miss you asking me to teach you how to breakdance, I miss you wanting to play basketball in the backyard, I miss you coming to my house for my moms special medicine for your cough, I miss everything about you! I look atmy phone everynight and hope to see nickygoombatz is calling and hearing you say "can I come over." I miss the nights we stayed up and talked about everything. I miss everything about you! I would give anything to hear your voice again, see you walk again, run, joke, laugh and cry again.I would do anything to protect you from your bad dreams again. I just miss you so much. You were truly an inspiration and brother to me and to so many others. There are so many emotions in my heart that its hard to put into words, but I have tried to stay away from doing this because I am afraid to say goodbye, but this wont be a goodbye! This will be my see you later!

I Love You p.s.

I cant wait to see you again and say

"We dont give daps. We give HUGS!!!"

Jon De La Rosa

loving friend and brother January - 31 - 2006

DEAR NICKY,

In this tough time ive had a lot to think about, not only you but how hard its gonna be to tell our new cousin ryan mele about how great you were he was so young when we lost you. Then i thought how greatful i am that i knew you as well as i did. And the one memory that i pictured is when i said to you "toys arent real there fake like santa!" but you being as great as you were wouldnt give it up you spent the rest of that after- noon trying to make santa seem real to me. Well yes that was long ago but its a great memory ill never forget among other memories. your never lost, or forgotten, i keep you alive through pictures, or memories that i have or that people have told me of. I love you very much and i just wanted you to know that never in 1 million years will i ever forget you or everything you tought me, you changed me for the better and im glad i was a lucky one to know you!

Love you 4eva gumba! Frank Archina Jr. cousin
January - 31 – 2006

To Nicky,

i am sorry that it has taken mem so long to write to you. everyday i would sit here and think about what to say to you. the truth is that i dont want you to really be gone. i wish you were sill here. i is you so much words cant even explain the pain that i feel evryday. people kep telling me that it will get easier and soon i will feel no pian only your memory

.but i dont believe them everyday gets harder then the last. i miss caling you to come with me to the nail salon, to go out on one of our dates, or just hearing you seing you or just have the feeling that i coud go and see you or call you whenever i wanted. you taught me so much. some things you taught me were not to get worked up over small things, how to always beieve something good will hppen and most of all how to be strong. after seeing ow much courage and strength that you had i know i can get through each passing day. i remember when one day i came to see you and hang out with you and hen it was time for me to leave i said goodbye and ten you told me that whenever i leave him or anyone i have to say i love you because you never know what is going to happen and that you always want to leave telling the person how you feel. the last words that me and you spke to eachother were "Ilove you". you were always there when i needed you wheher it was to go shopping with me or staying ith me when i didnt want to be home alone. i can remeber so many memories that i have of you i cant help but laugh at some of them. you were always there loking after me making sure that i was okay. you had those certain rules i ahd to obide by that you made very clear to me and you made sure they were clear to my mom also so she would tell you when i did something you didnt like. you were always trieing to get me in trouble to by telling o me or making something up that i did to you. but no matter how manytimes you got me in trouble you tried to get me out of it twice as many times. i remeber making you mashed potatoes and they were horrible but you ate the entire thing with a smile on your face just so i wouldnt feel bad. your heart was so big.

i realy miss you and i wish you were here. i wish i could have a feet war with you again or watch you fall asleep on my lap. there is not a day that goes by i dont miss you. i look at your pictures on my wall and all ovr my house and i tr to re-live each and every moment i spent with you in my head. i wish i could but everything i am feeling into words but it is impossible it took me so long to bring myself to write this. you are some- thing to rember and nothing to forget. your life was short and sweet but i am so gratefull to be a part of it and i know that you are a part of my life forever and you will always be watching over me to one day meet again.

i love you with all my heart and soul and i will never forget you you were my best friend

love always michelyn xoxoxo Michelyn close friend
February - 1 - 2006

Nicky,

I cant believe it has been a month since youv'e been gone. i think about you everyday. And i woneder if it will ever get easier.

I know you see the collage i have of you right when I walk into my room. This is the hardest thing i have ever been through. No one ever thought this day was actually going to come. We are all so used to you going into the hospital but then just weeks later speeding past us on 22. I never thought there would be a day when I would only have your memory, your pictures and your voice in my heart. I know you can hear me at night when i talk to you. when ever im by myself doing some thing stupid i always stop and think you can see me and you probably laughing at me. I think back on all our memories togethor and how much fun we used to have.

When we went to prom- the second we met ,up just pinning your flower on made us crack up. And then when we were there and we sat at a table and didnt know anyone so we made a deal that we each couldnt leave the table for more then 5 minutes. i can still hear your voice telling me how hott you were gonna look in your suit.

Or just past june when me, you, alexa, john, joelle, and jackie all went to mount fugi for my bday and how you and john got cut off from drinking anynmore sake by the waitor and all the funny pix we took. Or when me and dom came to your house bf DNA and you STILL weren't ready. or all the text messages we would send eachother of funny things at 2 in the morning. The times we would go eat at Cozi and that one time we were there you spilt the soda EVERYWHERE and i had to run to the bathroom because i was laughing to loud. and when you were in the bathroom i gave a girl your number and told her you liked her!! we had so much fun together. I cant believe just a two months ago i was watching i love the eighties with you and Miss Seventeen. if i would have known that that would one of our last times together i would have never left. i regret so much when you asked me to sleep over and i couldn;t because i had work ,that i didn't just call in sick. there were so many times i wanted to tell you how much i love you but i knew i would break down. The only way i could tell you was in letters so i would write you one anytimes something happened. i came to your house on eevery holiday to see you. I was just with you on christmas and i made everyone put santa hats on to take pictures. if i would have known you wouldn't be here four days later i would have told you how much you inspire me. we all go through shit and think its the end of the world when we brake up with someone or we have alot of school work, but you were going through something so hard and worse then anything we could ever imagine and never a peep came out of you. you never wanted anyone to feel bad for you . Nicky you truley were an amazing person. you have given me faith. You have given EVERYONE faith. . its just so hard for all of us left behind to grasp the fact that we will never be able to see you again. its not fair that someone so young had to go through what you went through. Its not fair that we cant go out with you anymore or have bbq's in the summer with you. Selfishly i wish you never had to leave but i know your in a better place right now. i know that times heals all wounds and hopefully one day i will be able to think of you with out sadness and tears and just happiness and smiles because that is what you would have wanted.

I love you so much Nicky,
Keep shinning down on us-
you will never be forgotten....
Caresse
Friend February - 1 - 2006

DEAR NICK...

Wow I know this is extremely weird, but being that i am a pretty private person im writing this to u (even though your never physically going to read it)because i cant display how i feel online or in a speech because the words hurt too much to say them outloud. I never got to tell you how I feel, Nick, and that hurts so bad. I always said to myself that I never wanted any regrets when the time actually came. I guess what happened was that in my heart I knew what was going to happen, but I just didn't want to believe it so bad that I felt like the time would never come. Also, I never wanted to make you feel uncomfortable. Me and you had a fun, always acting stupid, never serious kind of friendship and if I had one day come out of nowhere telling you all this it may have made you upset as well as me too.

Of course, now I wish that I had looked past it all and just went ahead and said everything i felt. Even though I didn't know you as long as you have known all of your other friends, I believe you were equally close to me as them. You were a very important part of my life. I thought about you every single day, even before you became really really sick. God , i was always so nervous and scared and I wanted to do something for you to just make everything disappear but that's not possible. And your personality! Where do u come from?? I've never met someone so funny, so nice, so UNSELFISH , yet so sick at the same time . You're so cool. I told everyone i knew about you.. not because i wanted them to sympathize, but to let everyone know that i know a great person who deserves the kudos and respect you've earned. I had so much fun knowing you Nick, so much. uugh this hurts.. i hate that i even have to do this to be honest. it's not fair.

Obviously you deserved a far better place than what you've endured that past 18 years of your life. I don't know too much about your family and your background, but i do know that your mom is a greatttttt person. It breaks my heart 100 times more to think that you two are not physically together right now. she loves you so much nick. i told her at the wake that i'll never leave her. i love your mom and i'll be there for her whenever she needs me. And the ladies who have been helping her throughout, they loved you just as much. I'm sorry that i don't have better words for you right now. This letter is making me cry and I can't think. You deserve a novel, but for some reason I can't get it all out. I dreamt that you walked into Heaven and you say Mikey and you said "whatup Nigga" and u guys gave each other a pound. I woke up crying.. but for the first time it was because i was truly happy you have found eternal happiness.. no more pain, no more sick...now you can walk...skip... run...oh God.. i'm really upset now.

Everyone knows that you deserve the kingdom you were granted a few weeks ago. and I know that you were sent to us all to teach us a lesson and boy Nick did u teach me a lot. You taught me that life is like a precious stone, or piece of jewelry or painting MANY PEOPLE MAY HAVE IT , BUT ONLY FEW SEE THE TRUE BEAUTY WITHIN IT. You taught me that people take advantage of their lives and that there is a billion times more to the superficiality that people live by. You taught me to hold friends and family close to me and showed me how special they are...you've taught me how to look at things more positively...you've helped me grow, mature, understand a lot of different things... But the one thing i don't understand is why you are not here. Someone like you deserves life as well as eternal peace...you deserve a wife and kids who love you ..hell even grandkids...but no...this wasn't it...you're in a beau- tiful kingdom now you're too good for here nick.

I am so blessed to have had you as my friend. I thank you with every- thing inside of me to have graced my life with your own. Hopefully, through me being a nurse (my inspiration was you by the way) I can meet many more beautiful souls, such as yourself, who will guide me through the journey of life, for it is very odd and at times hard. Im sorry i had not said this all before...however no regrets. Can't have that or i'll lose my mind. Plus there can't be any because just knowing you has been sufficient. I miss you...

Thank you, Nick, for being my friend, "partner in crime" and now my Angel. Love you "MahfutZ"!!

Love always..., A Special Friend Friend
January - 31 - 2006

NICKY

I miss you. I miss you so much, there are no words to describe it. You are on my mind ALL the time. I wonder if you can hear me when I talk to you. There are so many things that remind me of you; Songs I hear on the radio, Some of the songs on the computer. When I hear them I see you sitting at the computer listening to them while you're checking out the "My Space" site. I have pictures of you all over the house. I hold all that we shared close, and dear to my heart. I only wish I could have been able to take all your pain and suffering away. You were so strong and courageous. Nicky you were so much older than your 18 years.

You were always optimistic.

You had hopes for a great future, even though it seemed that life had dealt you a tough hand, to you it was "just another bump in the road", another obstacle to overcome. You NEVER gave up the fight. And what a fight it was. You did it so VALIANTLY! It only took you 4 years to teach so many SO much. I, for one, have a NEW appreciation for life, my family and loved ones. Your suffering was not in vain. You never complained.

NEVER once did I hear you say "why me?" Instead you used to say you were a miracle in the making.

Trust me you were, we just didn't know it at the time. The miracle is in these testimonials. Look at how many people NOW really appreciate ALL that God gives us, the good and the bad. For everything happens for a reason. Not one of us wanted to believe that we would lose you one day. But God decided that you had fulfilled your mission here on earth. I, as well as many others, TRULY cherish the times that we spent with you, and you will NEVER be forgotten. You ARE so SPECIAL. Yes Nicky, you deserve a novel, just like your friend said. I just wish the novel would have been a longer, happier one. With all the bells and whistles like you DEFINETELY earned and most of all deserved. How can someone so young have so much COURAGE, ENDURE so MUCH and still have the CHARISMA and the LOVE OF LIFE that you had? It's because that was the purpose that God gave you to us. To teach us how to appreciate the ones that we love, UNCONDITIONALLY, with ALL their faults!

I now believe that God borrowed you from HEAVEN and sent you to us to teach us this most valuable lesson. You were ALWAYS an ANGEL! You never got to get that tatto because you ALREADY had your ANGEL WINGS. Now you are back in your rightful place, watching over us and guiding us.

Lots of Love, ALWAYS
Yolanda

I LOVE AND MISS EVERYTHING ABOUT YOU. Theres not a day that goes by where I dont think about you... I miss the way you smile and even the way you laugh...

Your a true inspiration to me.Your the strongest person I know and that will never change... You were such a caring person and your ways will never be forgotten. You are a one and a kind kid and youve earned your wings... I know your in a better place now... I miss going to the hospital and visiting you almost everyday my memories with you will akways be cherished. (40 year-old virgin)

Love Always, Joelle 133*143

HELLO SWEETHEART. ITS ME. WELL HERE WE ARE, VACATIONING IN FLORIDA.

This is my first vacation without you and i feel like i am missing some- thing. and i am, you. i never realized how lonely you feel even when your not really lonely. yesterday i was laying outside next to Zio Franks pool and i put you out on the lawnchair so you could tan with me! sounds corny huh,we had fun though huh babe. i see what everyone writes to you and i feel as if there is not enough i can say to you. i think of all our memories together. i remember when you were little you thought you were the Ninja Turtles and you jumped off the couch and cracked your head open on the table...you didnt seem to feel a thing, or when we were playing with the kids upstairs and i thought i was tinker- bell and jumped off the picnic table and broke my leg.. daddy ran out in his towel...lol...remember? you were the handsomest man i ever knew! how is mikey? tell him i said "little italy" misses him very very much. i always think to myself that you can see everything im doing now, and in a way that puts me at ease. you are there when your not.i spoke to dominique last night. we had a nice talk about you...you know that already tho. tell Nonno i said hello and i miss him and cannot wait to see him. Until We Meet Again Baby.

I Love You. <3 xoxo

-you were not only my brother, you were my best friend and i admired you and your strength. you were one of a kind
Bianca

MY DEAREST SKIPPER, ANOTHER MONTH HAS PAST. EVERY MORNING I AM AT MASS [AS USUAL] RECEIVEING COMMUNION FOR YOUR INTENTIONS... THERE ISN'T A DAY THAT GOES BY THAT MY LITTLE ALTAR HAS A CANDLE LIT FOR U....YOU ARE WITH ME DAY AND NIGHT. ALSO NICKY, WHEN
YOU WERE 14 AND FOUND OUT THAT U WERE ILL, YOU IMME- DIATELY STARTED TO PUT UP UR ALTAR... OH !!!!!!!!!!!! HOW PROUD I WAS TO SEE WHAT YOU HAD IN MIND ALL THESE YRS THE GRACE OF GOD WAS LIVING IN YOU FROM THE BEGINING OF YOUR LIFE !!!!!!!!! SO UNTIL, NEXT TIME I WILL KEEP IN-TOUCH WITH YOU...MUCH LOVE AND HUGS !!!!!!!!!!!...EGGGIE--BIGIEEEEE BOOOOO
barbara feyl grandmother
February - 10 - 2006

WHERE HAS THE TIME GONE.? I FEEL LIKE ITS BEEN SO LONG SINCE YOU LEFT me. My heart is so sad without you here. it still doesnt feel real to me. for some reason i still feel you around me... i feel still you here.... yet my heart is still broken. And my mind is always occupied by sadness. I miss you more than u can imagine. I think about you all the time. Life is so hard... you had it bad. But as bad as you had it, you were so happy. I always ask myself how? how was he so happy?! and finally i see. You've showed me how to be happy...even when life is bad...because its too short to be mad, or angry, or upset...life is too short to hold grudges...and you never held a grudge... you had more friends than anyone i know... and you've inspired me to let go of my past...and be friends with people that i used to hate. Hate isnt in my vocabulary anymore...because life is too shorty nicky..and u didnt hate anyone. You showed me the real meaning behind alot of things i never saw.

i just wish i could see you one more time.. one more time, to thank you for all youve taught me..to hug you... to tell you how important you are to me... i dont think i ever really told you how meaningful you were..

although i told you i loved you all the time... i never fully expressed what u meant to me...and i regret that... but i know that now you know how important you are to me...and how loved u are.the last time i was in the hospital with you..was on a thursday night after i left school... we were by ourselves..and i was holding your hand...and your doctor came in and said "oh nickk is this your beautiful girlfriend?" and you and i looked at each other and laughed... and you said to the doctor "no, shes a really close friend though". those words that you said replay in my head all the time. it warms my heart knowing that i was "a close friend" to you. Although i already knew that. to hear you say it felt good.

i miss you nicky. i love you D February - 14 – 2006

HAPPY VALENTINE'S DAY MY SWEETHEART

Nicky, my love, my son, my supporter... Today is our second holiday away from one another. Five years ago on this date 2/14, you endured your first painful surgery (the removal of your tumor on your fibula). As I walked to you in the surgery room, you yelled out to me as I walked towards you, "Mommy, it hurts, did they get it all out?" My eyes filled with tears looking into your eyes and took a breath. At that moment I felt helpless, yet in the midst of what we were up against, God gave me the strength to take your hand and guide you through these last five years of your life with never-ending happiness, unconditional love, and precious days together. I never dreamed that my son would be taken so far away from me where I could not walk into your bedroom and watch you sleep, sing to you, hold you in my arms, listen to your loving ways you spoke to me, and the way you stood by me. Instead, the disease consumed our lives. I always thought I would see you playing basketball for your college, and then playing with your children. A sport you loved and looked forward to so much. My heart is suffering so much that it will never heal. My beautiful angel is gone from me forever. I will never hear your laugh again or see your beautiful smile. Months pass, I grieve quietly, crying alone. The dates on the calendar that were so important, are not anymore because I cannot share them with you. The daily routines are mundane so to speak, the pain is taking over. Everything reminds me of you and I cannot escape as the pain flows through my veins and sears my soul.

Oh God Nicky, where are you? I wait for you every day to come through that door. Somedays I just want to come see you but I know it would be wrong to do such a silly thing. No one will ever understand how I feel, you were the only person who honestly loved me for ME. You have completed me, Nicky, with your selfless behavior towards everyone you came in contact with. A trait in which you instilled in many, and for this, I thank you because you have made an impact on so many...

Thank you, God, for the Gift of my son, Nick
Luv, Mommy

HEY NICKY,

Words couldn't even delineate the young boy you were cause no words can possibly do the justice for how amazing you were. When I endeavor to describe you as a child and the memories I have shared with you, I get frustrated because those memories are too amazing for words. They are the memories that you feel in your heart, that make you laugh, that make you smile. When I started babysitting you, you and your sister became more than the kids I babysat, you guys became my friends, & my family. Each time spent with you guys touched my heart, was an adventure, a fun memory, a new laughing moment. I used to brag when I babysat for you guys and all my freinds who met you guys always wanted to come along. You radiated a room, your half-smirk smile, dreamy eyes and your sensitive-golden heart always made everyone want to be around you. I truly don't believe that any other babysitter in the world was as lucky as me. I would give up anything I was doing to spend time with you guys because you always knew how to wear your smile and make others smile along with you. Like I told you recently, no one has ever touched my heart as much as you did when you ran home, and up the stairs, swung the door open, with open arms flaring, gave me a million dollar hug, out of breath, but still managing to let out a few words of love. On that day, I was befuddled how a young boy was ableto show that kind of love. I looked up to you Nick. Of all the years I watched over you, you never complained, argued or made anyone around you feel less than 100%. Even back then, I would attempt to describe how amazing you were, but it almost seemed like you were too good to be true that I could never really explain how " " you were and even now I still can't find a perfect word to describe you. I don't think Websters dictionary has come up with a word to explain someone as special as you and it isn't going to be easy because you are truly one of a kind. Babysitting you and your sister wasn't a job, it was a priveledge. You guys taught me so much and gave me soo many memories that when it was time for you guys to watch yourselves, I wanted to turn back time, so I could watch you all over again. I still want to watch you guys!! I want to be that old babysitter because I truly love you guys and I was always soo excited and happy to be around you guys. When I think about having kids one day, I hope they are as caring, loving, adventur- ous, fun and beautiful like you and your sister. As I sit here typing, I am indulged in hapiness thinking about the times I shared with you guys--

A.H fair, crestwood pizza, watchin movies in ur moms room, Ramen noodle soup, pumpkin painting, don't forget the nite lite, reading to you, park, eewww tuna, sleepovers.....There are some memories that we utilize to escape into a world of hapiness, peace, love, genuiness, innocence, unfabricated joy and these memories are some of the hardest ones to obtain and thanks to you, you and your sister gave me these kind of memories.

Love you. Miss you. Justina
Friend/admirer February - 20 - 2006

HI NICKY BABE!

Today such a weight was lifted off my chest. Nicky, I want to share my experience with everyone close to our hearts. At first I was scared because I never did this before, but I was determined as my days are filled with so much sadness and pain. This evening will be never forgotten and I look forward to sitting with you again and again and when I feel like ending my life. You saved my life tonight. As many of you are aware, Nicky was a VERY spiritual angel. I took it upon myself to go online 5 weeks ago in search of a Ouiji board on eBay. I purchased it from a woman who was cleaning out her mother's attic. It is very old. It has been in a special place in our new apartment and today I used it. My friend was with me as we sat together and looked at each other as if "is this for real?" So I took a big breath and placed my fingertips onto the mysterious message indicator and began to ask questions. At first it was a jumble of letters, but I think you were on your way to sit with us. I asked the Ouija "where is Nicky" and it began to move slowly and I was asking it "who is Nicky with" I was so nervous I kept repeating myself going back and forth with those two questions and not giving it a chance to answer. So i took another breath and was calm, I said "Nicky are you here with us" and Ouija said YES and spelled out "SIT", so I assumed you were sitting with us. I asked you about the night you went to heaven and who took you, you spelled out MIKEY. I was in shock, in awe, unde-scribing words. I asked if Mikey was with you here with us and you said YES. At this moment I started to ball and cry with happiness I was getting choked up, and then you spelled out "EZ & L U", I just could not believe you were sitting next to me. You wanted Mommy to be easy(EZ) just as you always said to me when I was nervous or scared, you told me four times during our time together you loved me(LU) which I already knew but you gave me peace of mind that you were OK. At that moment it became easier for me to talk to you. You just kept talking to me through this Ouija board, it was the most incredible experience (besides having you) in my LIFE. Your sense of humor came out through our talk and I felt you coming into our new place and when you said GOODBYE. Nicky, I know now in my heart you are still alive and that you are with me every day guiding me because I also asked you "Nicky, I'm so lost every day, what do I do" and you spelled out the word WORK. It just kept flowing, the entire time I talked to you, we laughed together I can't explain it. I asked so many questions and we talked for 25 minutes. You told Mommy "YES" love your Pieta that you are in, and you also are happy with the fact you were "cremated" and not "buried in the cold dirt." I am so excited you are with Mikey and you have seen Grampa, but try to find little Gramma! You and Mikey are having a hell of a time together I am sure of it! I feel so much lighter knowing your really SAFE, people say words to comfort me but you know Mommy, I need to get to the nitty-gritty and I did that tonight, but I miss you so ****** much and knowing now how you saved my life tonight comforts my soul. It was emotional at first but when we got going, you made it feel as if you never left. You also told me you were going to St. Maarten with me in April and have been to Italy with Mikey. I cannot wait until we get down there and now Mikey will be able to come with us on all our trips! I am having diamond earrings and a ring made with your remaining ashes. As I stated in my other testimonials, I lived my life for you and I will continue to do so just as if we never parted. I have so many plans for us Nicky, just you wait and see!

I Love You my little pumpkin! Mommy

HEY BOO!!

i know you know how sad we all are that you are gone so instead of writing to you about the pain i feel, id rather from know on write to you only about funny memories. you know i love you, we all do, you know we all miss you so much, but it always makes me feel better to remember funny times and inside jokes we shared. Because your sickness NEVER got the best of you. Even when you were feeling your worst it was always a laugh. so today i will remember you about the time we went to the hospital so you could get radiation remember how hard we laughed when your dad almost hit that guy and we teased him about it all day!! and het was getting so mad lmao!! you were like "dad look out!!" and then he kept saying "that guys fine hes home eating dinner with his family! " yes i am sad but writing it to you wont change that, it wont fill the void in my heart- the only thing that does is my fond memories with you and all the funny things we did together.

i love you nicky and you jokes
will keeping me smiling forever....
Caresse

NICKY,

You are such a beautiful person. My memories with you go back to when you were about 8 years old. Those were the times when Little Ro and I would babysit you and your sister. You were such a pleasure to have around. You never gave us a problem, but you were that boy that would never give anyone a problem. Kind, Gentle, Respectful, Loving and Caring are words that come to me when I think about you. You are an AMAZING young boy who had such a positive energy on everyone.

God Bless You Beautiful Angel!

Love You, Roza

TWO MONTHS HAVE PASSED...

I will never understand...how you came into my life and left me with the limitless devotion & love you so freely exemplified.

I will never understand why you would always stand by me all these years without judgement.

I will never understand when people were cruel, you would overlook their """"ignorance."""""

I will never understand where your patience and strength came from.

You always protected me through the harshness in life with your guiding words of wisdom even as a child.

When you wrote on your website (myspace.com) last year, """""you will never be on my level""""" you knew what you were writing and hoping that others would take a cue on your inspiring words.

You and I both know Nicky the difference betwen an """""old soul and a new soul.""""" We are old souls, we have been here many times. You came here to teahch many lessons.Your no longer on an earth plane where we look upon one another with animosity, jealousy, judgement or even hatred. You have graduated and now in a place that is truly loving & free of pain. You tried your hardest to be the peacemaker, but more importantly, your antics displayed a soul of a true man with an honest heart.

It gives me comfort knowing that you always stuck by me from beginning to end. It gives me comfort knowing I experienced this wonderful love from someone who loved so selflessly...

My song I sang to you from when you were born as I rocked you to sleep at night until the night you left us,

LaLaLaLaLaLaLaLaLaLaLaLaLa, Nicky is a special angel sent from God above...Nicky is a little angel loved and cared by all, LaLa,La,La,La,La,La,La,La,La xoxoxoxoxox

Mommy

MY NICKY...

Mommy misses you so very much. From the moment I wake until I close my eyes, I know our connection is within our souls no matter where you are. As I grieve for you each day, I am getting through it. The daily visits & connections with you are overwhelming to mommy, yet knowing your safe in ways I never thought possible. The heavy blanket is lifting slowly & the sadness no longer exists. My heart knows where you are is safe. You are alive more than ever, working for me in heaven watching over Mommy.

Our soul connection will remain as I feel you, as I see you, and most importantly as I hear you every day, all day long talking to Mommy. You said to me last week, "Im so sorry Mommy, I wish things were different, my life may have been short but it was enriched by your unconditional love." Powerful words Nicky, I thank you for your loving guidance & protection.

Until we meet again, Mommy

NICK "BABE",

I cant believe that i havent seen your beautiful face or heard your voice. I wish i could see you one last time just to hug you and see you smile for one last time. It is so hard for me to write to you. For one i dont know what to say to you. I can never seem to put my feelings into words. And two i dont want you to be gone i dont want to write to you i want to talk to you. Its only ten days till i get to go on spring break and less then 3 months till prom. i am excited for both of these things to come but a part of me doesnt want it to. You told me you would come with me to my spring break and i wont get pictures with you from my prom you wont be there to see me graduate and you wont be there for after. I wish you were here so much. I love you sooo much and i miss even more. I will NEVER for get you. You were such a good person and you made so amny people smile just because you are you. i cant stop thinking of all of the time we spent together..our dates..our talks..all the memories. You ahve a special place in my heart and you will stay there for all of eternity. i miss you and think of you all the time and there are a million things that i see everyday that remind me of you. From a picture..to a movie..a certain creme..or even my den. There are so many things racing through my head right now i dont even no what to say. I cant wait to see you again.

i love you "babe" always and forever xoxox Michelyn Good Friend March - 29 - 2006

OFTEN WORDS GO UNSPOKEN, YET OUR WORDS WERE NEVER UNSPOKEN, WE always spoke the truth. The truth without judging, the truth through respect for one another. You held no grudges and would never betray your friends, loyal and true blue was this gift given to you. This is the uncommon bond that you and I shared, a bond in which no one will ever take from me nor rape from me the truth… I will only speak and feel at that moment. Only you Nick will understand the deepness of our souls. It is still quite difficult to get used to this new way of life, it will never be the same without you. Holidays are upon us and I am numb, people talk to me and I do not even hear what they are saying, I don't care what they have to say. By its very nature, life is a potpourri of events that are filtered through our emotional, physical, mental and spiritual selves. You appreciated these various aspects …you did with your experience through life's ups and downs which made you grow in the knowledge and wisdom as the loving and spiritual being you exemplified.

You accomplished this in a very short, yet a quite "complete" life. The love we share since your birth was strong enough to move the earth. You're by my side awake or asleep, now rest my love... your journey is through-

--everlasting life has been given to you.

I Love You Unconditionally, Mommy April - 2 - 2006

NICKY...ITS BEEN 3 MONTHS. MY MIND IS BROKEN.. MY HEART IS SHATTERED, but still, you're gone. YOU ARE GONE... those words haunt me. I cant believe how long its been since we've seen each other. i cant believe the last time we spoke to each other was 3 months ago. The last time we laughed...the last time we hugged.... i never thought there would be a last time. I thought you'd stay with me forever...
the last night i saw you.. I remember like it was yesterday.

i never thought it would happen to ME...never thought it'd be YOU. i couldnt believe that time had taken its toll, and it was taking you too. Your face was so swollen...but still as handsome as you've always been. You looked at me..and mustered up the words "Thank you so much ma" Your voice was weak and shaky. My heart fell to the floor... i tried to smile..but it was so hard...what i wanted to really do was throw myself on you and beg you not to go. Scream and cry..and ask God why he did this to you. Be angry that you were leaving me soon, but not accept it.

Be selfish enough to want you here forever. If only i got to tell you all the things i wanted to tell you. if only i would've allowed myself to break

down and REALLY cry to you..and tell you how i felt..and how much of and inspiration you were to me. It was so hard tho because i couldnt say all the things i wanted to say, without infurring that you were going to leave us. and i never wanted to face reality i never wanted to you feel as if you were dying i never wanted to treat you any different than any of our healthy friends...but i couldnt help it.. you were my LIFE, my purpose. After all the emotions that ran through my body after you said thank you so much ma..(at your xmas party your friends threw for you) we had a good rest of the night... it was short because u were so weak...but it was beautiful. Your friends were crowded you because no one could get enough of you. everyone loves you so much. At the end of the night...you went into your room to go to sleep...and i came in before i left to say goodbye to you... again you thanked me for everything...and quietly after i kissed you on your head...you said [a]love you...get home safe[o]... and that was it.... that was the last thing we said to each other before you flew away to heaven. i didnt see you for a couple of days after that...and then the night i was on my way to go to your house with veets,danielle,and bretty... i got the news.

I THINK ABOUT YOU ALL THE TIME. I TALK ABOUT YOU EVERYDAY. I EVEN FIND MYSELF TALKING ABOUT YOU TO PEOPLE I DONT KNOW. I FEEL LIKE EVERYONE KNEW YOU..AND IF THEY DIDNT..THEY SHOULD'VE.

BY BEING HERE...YOU LEFT AN IMPRINT ON EVERYONES

HEART...BY LEAVING, YOU LEFT A SCAR. Your presence still lingers here..and your voice plays clear in my mind. I wish i could just hear you once more...and know you're ok.

love you...get home safe

<3 dEe

HI NICKY SORRY I WASNT HERE ON THE 29TH.. I COULDNT GET TO A COMPUTER.IM HERE AT MOMMYS..IM ABOUT TO GO TO THE CITY TO PICK HER UP SHES HAVIN AN ATTACK AGAIN..HEHE..I MISS YOU PUMPKIN.. AND WE WONT MENTION THE TATOO THING.. ITS OK.. I LOVE YOU AND MISS YOU XOXO I CANT WAIT TO MEET YOU.. I CANT BELIEVE ITS BEEN 3 MONTHS

FEELS LIKE FOREVER! I MISS YOU
I LOVE YOU..XOXO UNTIL WE MEET AGAIN <3
BIANCA SISTER AND FRIEND March - 31 - 2006

NICKY,

OH NICKY I CAN'T BELIEVE IT'S BEEN THREE
MONTHS SINCE YOU LEFT US. THREE VERY LONG
MONTHS. SOMETIMES IT SEEMS LIKE YESTERDAY
WE WERE ALL TOGETHER, AND AT THE SAME
TIME, IT FEELS LIKE AN ETERNITY SINCE I LAST
SAW YOU. I FIND COMFORT KNOWING THAT YOU
WILL NEVER AGAIN FEEL PAIN. THAT YOU ARE IN
SUCH A SPECIAL, BEAUTIFUL PLACE. NOT A DAY
GOES BY THAT YOU ARE NOT IN MY PRAYERS, AND
IN MY THOUGHTS. I MISS YOU SO MUCH NICKY.
YOUR FACE AND YOUR SMILE ARE ETCHED IN MY
MEMORY. SOME DAYS I THINK OF YOU AND I
SMILE, OTHER DAYS ARE NOT SO GOOD: BUT I
CAN'T BE SELFISH; I KNOW THAT YOU ARE HAPPY
WHERE YOU ARE, THAT YOU ARE AT PEACE, AND
OUT OF PAIN FOREVER. I JUST WISHED WE HAD
ONE MORE CHANCE. I'M SURE THAT YOU KNOW
HOW MUCH YOU ARE LOVED AND CHERISHED,
BUT I WISH I HAD ONE MORE OPPORTUNITY TO
TELL YOU AGAIN. I HOPE YOU ARE ENJOYING
THOSE BIG BEAUTIFUL WINGS THAT YOU SO
RIGHT- FULLY EARNED, AND DESERVE. NICKY, I
FEEL SO PRIVILEGED TO KNOW A SPECIAL ANGEL
IN HEAVEN, YOU. ALWAYS WATCH OVER US. I MISS
YOU TERRIBLY.

LOTS OF LOVE YOLANDA
March - 29 - 2006

NICKY,

Rocco and I are better people because of you. Like I

told you when they went to get "i panini..." you put it all into perspective. Who cares about the trivial things in life? If everyone was as pure and inspirational as you, the world would be perfect. Thank you so much for making my world a little bit better. Thank you for allowing us to be a part of your life and thank you for making me feel like a cugina from day one. Ci vogliamo tanto tanto bene. Manchiamo voi più e più ogni giorno e siete per sempre nei nostri cuori.

    Jacq

I WILL ALWAYS REMEBER MY COUSIN NICOLA AS MY TWIN. I'M NICOLA'S older cousin Rocco Archina, everywhere he and I went we always were asked if we were brothers because we showed alot of resemblence. We eventually got fed up to the point where we did not want to keep saying we were cousins so we fooled many into believing that we were brothers, and that is a gift that will always stay with me. On belhalf of myself and all my freinds here in the United States Air Force I want to say that Nicola Mele will always be our Angel watching over us. God bless.

    Rocco A

"LOST SON"

    God has taken you away to be by His side. When I first saw, I cried and cried. Everyone tells me time will heal, yet they really have no clue how I feel. Time has come and gone since you went, sleepless nights and lonely days are what I have spent. Somehow I know we'll meet again, how, where, why, or even when, is the question I have deep in my heart during this time we are apart. Our love goes on in a different way but remember my precious son, for you, I still pray. When my time has come to be with you, My soul will be at peace.

    Love, Mommy

HELLO SKIPPER, I AM HERE WITH MOM. I DROVE DOWN {54 N HIGH ST}...SHE HAS A LOVELY APT. VERY NEAT. I WOULD LIKE TO SHARE THIS WITH YOU NICKY! THE ONE SIDE OF THE WALL IS ALL ABOUT YOU! MOM, HAS DONE A BEAUTIFUL DISPLAY OF YOU FROM TIME OF BIRTH TIL NOW...ALSO, YOU MAY BE AWAY FROM US! !BUT YOUR ''SPIRIT IS HERE"

! THAT IS WHAT IS IMPORTANT... AND, HOW MANY TIMES DID I TELL YOU... THAT THIS WORLD WAS ONLY TEMPORARY !! ANYWAY, YOU ARE ALREADY IN 'HEAVEN'... WITH OUR LORD"" ...YOU WENT STAIGHT TO HEAVEN [NO QUESTIONS ASK] BECAUSE U KNEW HOW STRONG YOUR 'FAITH WAS'" YOU WERE

VERY VERY SPECIAL, even FROM the time of conception !!!!!!... NICKY...many are 'called but, few are chosen I WILL ALWAYS BE PRAYING FOR you and Sissy .!!! until my last breath

!!TIL WE MEET AGAIN LOVINGLY, YOUR GRAM

HEY SWEETIE...

You now live through us, Your smile lights the way, Your eyes guide us,

Your memories keep us strong, Your spirit gives us courage, You're forever in our hearts.

That is the poem Michelyn wrote for you that was published in the 2006 Eastchester High School yearbook. She misses you so much espe- cially now. You two had so many plans for this time of year. I know you are here guiding her, thank you. Xox

---

IT'S BEEN ALMOST 5 MONTHS SINCE YOU WENT AWAY. I KNOW YOU ARE HERE in Spirit but I miss that sparkling smile, I miss you. You are an Angel Nicky so you spread those wings and fly!!!!! Your time here on this earth was short, too short, but your memory will live on forever. You were a gift, a treasure, one of a kind jewel that we were so blessed to have known you and shared in your life.

Love and miss you , till we meet again. Xoxoxoxxo
Jackie

TO MY CHILD

I always smiled when I saw your face and laughed when I felt like crying. I always let you choose your clothing and smiled when I saw how perfect your choice was..., I always stepped over my laundry to pick you up and take you to the park. I always left the dishes in the sink and watched you put your puzzles together as you taught me precious moments of "quality, loving time together". We would blow bubbles in the backyard/porch and I would never yell or grumble when you would scream for the ice cream truck when he came by. I never "worried" about where you were going or who you were going with or second guess your decisions. I would always let you roll my rum balls and help me back Christmas cookies for all our friends and family and never tried to "fix" them. You would have not one but two Happy Meals from Mc Donalds so you could have both toys. I would always hold you in my arms and tell you stories when you were born and how much your life meant to me. You would always splash in the tub, making a mess and I would never get angry. I would snuggle with you for hours as we watched TV/Movies as I ran my fingers through your beautiful hair and thank God that He has given me the greatest gift ever as I kissed you good- night, and gave you a squeeze, tighter and tighter, it is then I thanked God for you, and ask Him for nothing, except for ONE MORE DAY. There are no more days now that you are gone...loneliness creeps within as I wake up and go to sleep. Memories will NEVER prevail the pain inside of mommy...no one will ever understand a lost child.

Mommy

WHAT'S UP NICKY. I'M WRITING THIS TO WISH YOU A HAPPY BIRTHDAY, AND let you know how much I miss you. Remember us on 364, and how crazy we used to be? We shared so many great memories, that I will never forget. You were much more than just a friend to me, you were my brother. Maybe not by blood, but by many more things. We talked to each other about everything, and anything for hours on end. You were there to make me feel better whenever I was down. You came with me to that sweet 16 just because you knew I didn't want to go by myself. You were the best person I could have ever known in my life, and glad I met you. You truly were a gift to me, and many others. I miss you bro, and I wish it was like it used to be again. I'm still waiting for you to call me to come stay over since you lived here, and go on the computer to space all night, to go to bed at like 4, then to stay up talking till like 6. I know it will be like that one day again. I still feel you, smell you sometimes, which reminds me that you may not be here in the physical, but defi- nately still with us spiritually. We will meet again bro.

Love you and happy birthday, Chris

NICKY,

I won't lie to you kiddo, I have been hurting lately. Emotionally, phyisically, mentally. It hurts knowing that you are not here. I see your face every single day on my computer in this dungeon they call Korea. I feel trapped sometimes being in the Armed Forces and I feel very hypo- critical. God says thou shalt not kill, and I train everyday to take a life. I hate that thought, I feel I'm sinning by being here. You know Nick, I have been thinking lately how much we were together when we were little kids. Do you remeber our sleep overs? We used to drive our parents nuts over the sleep overs. I'm laughing right now because I was thinking how you, your sister, and I used to make fun of your dad with his accent and all. That was the good times kiddo. I also regret when you and Bianca left to move to the city, I felt like I lost you. I was broken all the times we got toghether at nonna's for x-mas, or easter, or any other gathering. When your father would tell us he was going to the city to pick you up, I would get so excited. It would give me butterflies man. I remeber we would go to that haunted house right down the road from my house. That was funny, I used to tell you and ur sis it was haunted. It never was man, I just liked scaring you and Bianca, it was so nice laughing with you guys. It makes me feel good sitting here at work, just typing to you. I actually feel like I'm talking to you, and deep inside, I feel like you can hear me for some reason. I cry sometimes to myself when I think of certain things. My alltime dream in life besides having a beautiful wife, is (as corny as it sounds Nick) to hold a simple piece of gold. To lift the FIFA World Cup trophy and play pro-soccer. I have never tried for a major team before, and hope to when I get to Italy. Nick, you knew how passionate I was, I have been playing semi-pro for a while now and am ready to move up. The reason why I,m telling you this buddy is because I knew some of your dreams, and compared to mine, mine seem dumb. A dream for me would to have you with me in Italy watching me play soccer. I realize the little things in life don't matter. I want you to know that from here on out, every single time I score a goal in any kind of game or practice, I will dedicate it to you. That is the least I can do for missing out on your teenage years with you. I'm just glad to know you had such great friends that took care of you. I wanted to attend your 18 B-day party so bad, but I was busy fighting terrorists, as much as that was not as important as missing out on you man. I ask you as a friend, cugino, brother, watch over some people for me. I know you are pretty busy up there, and not sure if you can watch over everyone, but watch over your parents man. I'm sure your mother must be taking things pretty hard, I want nothing bad to happen to her, and your father, God only knows what he is going through. I wish only the best of health to the members you loved the most. Your sister Bianca as well. She loved you more than anything. I know how much the family loved you. I see your freinds love you especially Danielle. She seems like she is not doing well emotionally. I ask you to please watch over all of us Nick because it is too hard being here without you. I believe in God, Jesus, and Madonna, but what I don't understand is why he took you so early, I can't be anymore selfish because I know you are better off where you are at. I cannot tell you enough how bad I miss u and how much I love you Nick, as soon as I get home I'm gonna hang out with your pops, and make sure he is ok. I will visit with your sister and see how she is doing. Well I should stop writing you now, I don't want to hog up the board. You are a true champ man, nobody can ever fill your shoes, I know everyone tells you that but believe me, you are so strong, you have a spirit that is unusual, a personality that makes everyone smile, a smile that makes people wonder if you were put on earth for a reason. You are undescribable man, I just am lost with how to express to you how wonderful you are. If I had one wish right now besides you being here, it would have been to sleep over with you that night I visited you. I remeber your back hurt and Zia Toni was messaging it and I helped you to the bathroom. I did not stay with you that night because my father had no way of getting home. I wish I had stayed over that night because it would had been a privelage to stay on the couch with you and hear you breath while you slept. Nick stay handsome brother, and don't nag the ladies too much, I love you like my brother and someday we will be reunited like boys again. You keep watching over us like the angel in heaven that you are.

Your cugino Rocco Archina

JULY - 28 - 2006
Oh, My Nicky...
There is no more need to express the man you are or

exemplified on this earth. Courageous.

Yes, we all miss you and hold fond memories of your quirky and ways, yet what we hold special in our hearts is you set an example to those who one day will prevail whatever obstacles may come their way. You're the "MAN"

I am so proud of you, proud of the man you became in such a short lifetime. Your wisdom was astounding. Mommy misses you so very much, my days are long… and nighttime I sit wait for you to come home so I can feed you and pounce on you about "where you were" "who you were with" yes, I was nosey, but you LOVED it! Now, I know your safe, and watching over all of us. I feel you all around me every minute of the day.

I Love you, Nicky, more than life itself. Mommy.

NICKY,

Hey bro do you remeber when we were young and we would wres- tle? I always used to kick your ass? LOL. How are you today kid? I'm listening to a song that reminds me of you right now. It is by one of our guys, Nek from Italy. It is called Quando non ci sei. It means when it isn't there. It reminds me of you because I refuse to believe that you left, so my thought of you being gone isn't there. Di parliano di te, I talk to you even though you physically are not here. It is like everything reminds me of you. See this time in ourlives would have been great. I'm going to the motherland in 9 months, living in a beautiful big house that is free, on the water of our home town man. I get so depressed about that thought because I feel selfish going there and enjoying life without you. I swear man, we would have lived toghether, I'd teach you Italian, and I'd take you out and get ya a gorgeus Italian girl. (I know you wouldn't need my help or anything like that). Well I'm just sitting here at work this is the last day of our excercise, then we go back to regular shifts. The people I work with are great, but it is a tough, rewarding, demanding life. Never thought I would see the world man. You and I would play Gi Joes when we were younger, and these fighting games. We had a great childhood toghether, I just cannot believe I missed out on your teenage years, I regret that so bad. Everytime I go home I hang out with Rocco Mele and Ralphy. I do not ever want anything to happen to them and regret not hanging out with them. We had our own crew man, it was always us 4. You and I would walk around and people would call us Arabs because were exotic looking. Ha Ha. That makes me laugh. I hope you were never upset with me for missing out on your older years as a young man. Like I said man, when god says he is satisfied with my mission here on earth, we will meet again and make up for lost time.

Rocco

Nicola,

How was ur weekend? Mine was ok, Jackie is leaving this coming weekend, and I shall be alone once again. I don't do to well alone. Not trying to feel sorry for myself it is just me. I'm too family oriented to be by myself. It sucks. But sacrifice is a huge part of our lives. I'm sacrificing me being here in Korea, so that I can go to a beautiful base in Italy. That is how this buisness works, you give them a year here, you get base of choice after that. But oh well that is life I should not be complaining. I talked to your mom through email Nick, glad to hear she is doing well. I hope to see her and some of your friends this December when I go home. It will be hard seeing your residence where you used to be, but reminis- cence is always good. Letting out feelings is a real man. I cry when I need to, that is natural. I wanted to apologize that I have not emailed you in a few days. I have been busy this weekend with helping Jackie getting ready to leave and all. You know I noticed this weekend, I find it easier when I think of you, I go outside and listen to music, songs that you liked, songs in Italian that remind me of you, that helps alot. Well I will get back to work now, I wish I could sit here all day and just email you, that is the only time I feel good lately. Maybe someday my pain will heel a a little better as time goes on, but only a fool who knew you would forget you, as long as you stay in my head, there will be a little pain there. Love you kiddo, talk to you tomorrow morning.

Your big cousin,
Rocco Archina Cugino July - 28 - 2006

GOOD MORNING MY BOY,

It is Rocco. The weather here sucks right now. We are in monsoon season. Rain rain rain. Sometimes that s good though, it feels nice. How is life in paradiso? I'm sure wonderful. Well I'm keeping my word buddy, tryng to stay in touch wth you once a day. Jackie and I are going to go downtown and shop around for our new Jerseys for the new season. These guys did not want to get Italia jerseys because they do not have the courage to wear a champion shirt, so I picked the 2nd team on the list, Brazil. That s our team name, but you know I play for u and our hometown, Italia. I got a game Monday against the Koreans, I play defense so I may not score, but if I do, look down on me, becuase I will be lookng up at you. Each goal I score is a kiss to you buddy. I miss you soooooooooooo much man. Why did you have to go? You were too beautiful to leave. Sorry I know that is selfish, u stay where u are, ur pain free kid. Ur 18 years on earth impacted everyone, people who even did not know you. Know that phrase when one says "I believe angels roam the earth", they were talking about you nick. That is the truth, not just spit- ting out words, its true. You never even harmed a bug man, that is why I think you are where u are. God takes the great ones man, this earth is hell, his angels do not belong in hell, but like Jackie said, ur body is the only thing missing, I know you are next to me right now while Im typing tellng me to stop jacking up my spelling. Ha. I love you bro, not a SECOND, A SECOND that u leave my mind, on the soccer pitch, in the bathroom, at work, on the field training, in my house, outside, listening to music, fighting with my wife, fighting with myself, sleeping, staying awake, working out at the gym, calling family at home, drinking coffee, going out, watching TV, playing vdeo games, sitting listening to music, emailing people, going to the movies, going for a jog, crying, laughing, joking, being healthy, being sick......on.....on. and on. My point is I'm just lost wth words man. I cannot express to you or anyone how much I miss you. What I would give up to hug you once more and tell you "Nick, I love you, please let me help you take away ur pain". The best memory I will cherish 4-ever with you is watching that beautiful smile when you would look at me make fun of your fathers accent. I think of how you used to die laughing when I would mock ur father. Sleep well kid and have a gorgeus day up there, watch over all of us. You are considered my brother for all eternity.

Your cousin, ROCCO ARCHINA

NICOLA,

Per favore, lo so che ai tante cosi a fare cho paradiso. Ma cugino ta ha bisogno di l'aiuta tua. Lui senta mala senza tia. Per favore, solo una notta viene cho il sogni soi. Lui ti vuola tanto tanto tanto bene e si spagna di muorenda. Dici a lui che tutti e buona con tia cho paradiso. E ha bisognio u confidence a fare u cosa giusta per noi. Ayutalo. Lo so che ido sapa che vuola fare, ma ha paura. Da pace a menta sua. Mo, speriamo che tutti e buona con tia. Ti voglio tanto tanto bene, e ti mancho. Penso di ti ogni giorni bello. Stati buona, angelo mio. Grazie per tutti sacrificie che facisti.

Con amore per sempre, Jacq

NICKY...MY LOVE...YOU COME TO ME IN SO MANY WAYS AND TODAY WAS THE worst! As I was sitting at the Caffe I saw this old man walking towards me. He had your brace on his right leg, just as you wore every day. He was walking just like you. He had a dropped foot. I noticed his right leg to be thinner than the other, just like yours. He walked into the Caffe and came out and sat at the table facing me directly, sat down, and smiled. I couldn't bear to look at him anymore. I took a breath and looked at him again. He had on a NY Yakee cap, exactly as you wore it. This old man was simply sitting face to face with me enjoying this beautiful day, yet I was cringing inside. My hands started to shake. I had to get up and go inside. Before I did, I approached this man and said "May I ask you a question?" He said yes sure. I asked him what happened to his leg, he proceeded to tell me he has been wearing his brace for twenty years. He had a rare form of Polio. He then asked me "Why do you ask?" At that moment I broke down with tears and said you remind me of my son who is no longer with me, he wore the same brace, on the same leg with the same thin appearance like you, in addition, you're wearing his favorite baseball cap. He almost choked and said he was so sorry. I said it's ok, your just a reminder that my son is always around me and I walked into the Caffe. My friend Diane saw my flushed face and gave me a hug. But this is not the end of my experience today. As I was leaving, an old very very old man came into the Caffe and asked if one of the customers dropped this money he showed me all rolled up. I said I don't think so sir, I think it is yours now. This old man also reminded me of you. He was wearing a white "cap" not a LaCoste but the exact cap you wore. His antics we so pleasant and peaceful just as the man with the brace. Nicky, every day does not get easier for Mommy, it only gets worse, yet, I know in my heart your free of pain and your love was not of this earth. Reminders of the man you were and examples you have made, is why mommy is so very proud of you. No degree or job will ever equal what you have endured in your lifetime.

Love... Mommy

HI NICKY,

I can't believe it's almost 8 months. I feel like this is all a bad dream and you will walk through the door and tell us it was one of your prac- tical jokes as usual. I guess that is really only a dream to wish that. I wish it can happen because everyone misses you so much. We never stop talking about you. We all hate the number 29 for what it represents. It gets sadder and sadder the closer to the date. I don't think that will ever change. I know your happy in heaven with God . I guess we are all alittle selfish to be sad cause your not here. I guess it's ok for everyone to be alittle selfish because we will never stop missing you.

Love,
Ann Marie September - 7 - 2006

SOOO IM IN THE CAR WITH MY PARENTS TODAY ON 2ND AVENUE AND I HAD MY eyes closed the whole time thinking about you (because that end of the city reminds me of you..) so about 20 minutes or so goes by without me opening my eyes... and my dad stopped short.. so i opened my eyes , and right infront of me was a restaraunt on the corner called NICK'S . in hugeee letters, there was ur name staring at me.
i smiled because it was so ironic. i knew it was you...
<3 i love you

MY NICKY POO, I AM JUST SO AMAZED OF THE INCREDIBLE SOUL YOU are...two months before you went to heaven you sat up in your hospital bed and looked over at me and said ªMaº you know what? I said what Nicky (assuming a wise remark will only come out of your mouth cause your humor and cracks never ended! yet instead you were looking pretty serious) you said ªwatch Bianca's gonna get pregnant! I said WHAT????? your nuts! you were dead serious shaking ur head saying Bianca is gonna get pregnant.º Well my dear, you were right. Our family is going to be blessed with a baby boy very soon. I am so looking forward to this blessed celebration, how funny that God works in mysterious ways. And you know, we will persevere in whatever comes our way. I thank God every day all day long how blessed I was to give birth to both you and your sister. It is all coming together now that I see life's plan laid out in front of me. I understand more and more each day. My faith pulls me through each day that I cannot see you. But I know you're with me and u live within me for the things I have been able to do all these months without you by my side. Bianca is doing so well and I know you're proud of her acceptance into "Maria College." She started her next semester towards her nursing degree. Her goal is to continue onto medical school and study in the field of oncology. I talk to her every other day, she has matured so very much. You made such an impact on your sister and I love you both so very much.

Luv, Mommy xoxox

NICKY,

HOW IS IT POSSIBLE THAT WE HAVE BEEN WITHOUT YOUR BEAUTI- FUL SMILE FOR 9 MONTHS. IT STILL SEEMS SO UNREAL TO ME. WE ARE ALL MISSING YOU DESPERATELY. WE ALL KNOW THAT YOU ARE IN A MUCH BETTER PLACE, BUT WE ARE SELFISH AND WISH WE HAD YOU HERE WITH US. NICKY, I HOPE SOME- WHERE, SOME HOW, YOU KNOW WHAT A SPECIAL PERSON YOU ARE. YOU TOUCHED OUR HEARTS, AND LEFT YOUR SMILE ETCHED ON IT. I WILL NEVER FORGET YOU. I PRAY THAT ONE DAY WE WILL BE REUNITED AGAIN, AND WHAT A GLORI- OUS DAY THAT WOULD BE. I'M GOING TO GIVE YOU THE BIGGEST HUG AND KISS!!!!!!!!!!!!!!!!!!!!!!!!!!! I MISS YOU NICKY. COME AND VISIT ME IN MY DREAMS.

LOTS OF LOVE ALWAYS YOLANDA

MISS U SEPTEMBER - 29 - 2006

Today is nine months since you left us... i feel like a broken record everytime i say its so unreal...but thats the only thing i can express in words...everyone is forever heart broken nick, its just not fair... your out of pain and an angel watching over us now... thats what we need to tell ourselves,, not that it takes any of the pain away. your spirit is still here, just keep watching over and let us know ur here...

i love you Nick ~ Dom

R.I.P. NICKY ~ UNTIL WE MEET AGAIN GOOMBATZ THIS IS FOR YOU...

I never got to tell you nick

How much you meant to me I never got to tell you for the fear of what that'd mean,To tell you what you meant to me I'd have to face the fact

That one day you'd be leaving And I couldn't handle that This may be late but I think you knew How much I loved you nick

How glad I am to have had our time Even though it was too quick You always knew just what to say and always gave me strength

I wish I'd told you I loved your laugh Your smile, your spirit, your way There's so much now I wish I'd said Instead of kept inside

I wish I got to tell you Nicky When you were still alive Whenever I watch scarface Nick I'm gonna think of you And when the Yankees have a win

I'll cheer for them for you Nick your memory will never fade I know this for a fact You were the strongest man I'll ever know But I know Nick, you knew that I love you... your always in my heart... everyday... everyday

Jessica, Your Cousin

MOMMY

October - 28 - 2006

HAPPY HALLOWEEN MY NICKY POO. THIS WEEKEND IS MOST DIFFICULT FOR ME. HALLOWEEN WAS YOUR FAVORITE HOLIDAY BECAUSE YOU WERE THE BIGGEST PROFESSIONAL PRANKSTER. I REMEMBER ONE YEAR WHEN I DRESSED YOU AND SISSY UP. SHE WAS WEDNESDAY FROM THE ADAMS FAMILY AND YOU WERE JACKIE "O". AND WHEN MOMMY TOOK YOU TO SALEM MASSA- CHUSETTES AND SISSY WAS SO CUTE, SHE WORE THE PINK FELT SKIRT W/ THE POODLE ON IT FROM THE 50'S. AND YOU WERE A PUMPKIN. OH AND LET'S NOT FORGET YOUR SPIDERMAN COSTUME FROM NYU. YOUR LONG SLENDER LEGS OH HOW FUNNY YOU WERE, IT WAS SO DAM TIGHT AND HOW U WERE PROUD OF THAT BODY, NOT TO MENTION YOUR PACKAGE! LOL. WHEN YOU WERE 11 I TOOK YOU TO THE REAL AMITYVILLE HOUSE ON HALLOWEEN, AND YOU BOTH WALKED UP TO THE DOOR FOR "TREATS". AS YOU WALKED BACK TO ME I TOOK A PHOTO OF YOU & WHEN I DEVELOPED IT, THERE WAS A WHITE LIGHT ALL AROUND YOUR LITTLE BODY. BUT AS YOU GOT OLDER YOU LOVED TO PLAN YOUR HALLOWEEN WITH YOUR FRIENDS, EGGING, THE TOLIET PAPER, SHAVING CREAM...ON YEAR THE COPS WERE CHAS- ING YOU AND YOU JUMPED OVER A FENCE AND SCRAPPED UR LEG VERY BADLY, BUT YOU NEVER GOT CAUGHT! THAT'S MY BOY˜! "MR. SMOOTHY" I CAN'T IMAGINE WHAT YOU WOULD HAVE DONE THIS YEAR IF YOU WERE HERE, YOU ALWAYS HAD THE PLAN TO DO SOME CRAZY SHIT. DON'T YOU WORRY, MOMMY WILL MAKE UP FOR YOU. I KNOW YOUR GOING TO EX- PERIENCE A WONDERFUL

HALLOWEEN WITH MIKEY, CARL, GUERMO & STEVEN. YOUR NOT ALONE MY BABY. LUV U MORE THAN LIFE ITSELF, MOMMY

NICKY,

Rocco and I were walking last night and I said to him..." can you believe Nicky has been gone for almost a year?" He said..." no...no I f****** can't." Nicky we never thought that we would be having that conversation. I think about that night that you slipped away. We miss you so much and we are thankful to get to dream about you every now and then. Please continue to watch over Zio Nick, your mom, Bianca, Isabella, Nonna, Gram, and your nephew. I miss you so much and your death is not yet a reality but you have taught me so much.

It has been quite a year for Rocco and I but I feel like I can finally breathe. I think we went over the waterfall, and now we are sailing along in the "Pond of Peace." Watch over your cousin Rocco and please help him to make all of his dreams come true. Thank you so very much being our angel and even though Rocco doesn't always get time to write, we look at your picture every day and smile bittersweetly. Please give everyone who loves you so much, the strength to get through these holi- days, celebrating your life and not mourning your death. We love you so so so so much. Words cannot express...

Jacq

HI NICKY,

I started Christmas shopping alittle. It was sad, it brought back reminders of what we were all doing last year at this time. Wondering if we could get you home for the holidays. You wanted so badly to have thanksgiving home, and you did. It was only for the day, but it made you so happy. Your mom & gram & friends would have moved the earth to get you home.

Well, I just wanted to tell you that I'm thinking of you every day. You will soon become an Uncle. I know Bianca will tell your nephew all about you, and how wonderful you were. He had the best Uncle ever. Now he has an angel for an uncle. You are an angel Nick.

Love,
Ann Marie Nov. 12, 2006

HI NICKY BABE.

i was sitting here reading all the things people write you and it makes me so sad. i have missed you more than ever lately, im not sure why. i was thinking about the past, and i miss the way you used to stay in the bathroom for hours*just doing your hair*. and how you would tease me about everything... "keep eating bianca" ...hehe.

i miss you teaching me things...like how to steal moms vodka*take some out*put water back in! (sorry ma). but most of all, i miss just being able to pick up the phone and call you, cuz i loved to hear your voice on the other end of the phone. your nephew is going to be here very soon, and i am so upset to kno that he cannot meet you. he would have loved to. but he will see you soon. watch over him and guide him through. we love you and miss you very much. no goodbyes, we will see you later.

Bianca 11/9/2006

HAPPY THANKSGIVING MY DARLING...,

LAST YEAR AT THIS TIME I WAS PREPARING FOR YOUR THANKSGIVING DINNER. NEVER DREAMING IT WOULD BE OUR LAST THANKSGIVING TOGETHER. ALTHOUGH YOU WERE IN THE HOSPITAL, MOMMY MADE EVERY EFFORT TO MAKE SURE YOU CAME HOME FOR THE AFTERNOON. DR. RAUSEN ALLOWED YOU TO

COME HOME FOR 6 HOURS VIA AMBULANCE. YOUR WALKING ABILITY WAS COMING TO AN END BUT YOU WERE STILL DETERMINED TO FIGHT NO MATTER WHAT. AS YOU SAT IN YOUR WHEELCHAIR IN FRONT OF THE TINY TABLE IN THE LIVING ROOM, YOU ASKED MOMMY TO BRING OUT THE TURKEY SO YOU COULD LOOK AT IT. AS YOU STARED AT THE TURKEY, TEARS STREAMED FROM YOUR EYES. AS I WATCHED YOUR EMOTION I FELT HELPLESS BUT I COULD NOT LET YOU SEE MY PAIN. GRAMMA MADE YOUR FAVORITE "MASHED POTATOES" BUT YOUR APPETITE WAS NOT THE GREATEST, YOU WERE VERY WEAK. CARESS CAME BY TO SPEND SOME TIME WITH YOU. TODAY I WENT BACK TO OUR OLD APARTMENT TO SEE YOUR ROOM. THE PERSON WHO LIVES THERE WAS NICE ENOUGH TO LET ME IN. I CRIED A LITTLE BUT IT WAS NOT THE SAME, I KNEW YOU WERE NOT THERE BUT SUBCONSCIOUSLY I WAS LOOKING FOR YOU. MOMMY IS SO GRATEFUL FOR HAVING YOU IN MY LIFE. YOU WERE INSPIRING AND CREATED A LEGACY THAT WILL LIVE FLOAT THROUGH ETERNITY. I SIT HERE IN AWE OF YOUR SPIRIT AND UNSELFISHNESS. I HAVE NOT MET ANYONE YET THAT HAS ONLY A SMALL PERCENTAGE OF YOUR CHARACTER. YOU ALWAYS HAD THE UTMOST RESPECT. I MISS YOU SO MUCH NICKY BECAUSE YOU WOULD NEVER LEAVE MOMMY ALONE ON A HOLIDAY. I WAS GOING TO TAKE UP GRAMMAS INVITE FOR TURKEY DINNER BUT IT IS A TENDER AND EMOTIONAL DAY FOR OUR FAMILY AND I CHOOSE TO BE WHERE I WAS LAST YEAR WITH YOU. OUR FAMILY WILL NEVER BE THE SAME WITHOUT YOU. LOVINGLY, MOMMY

OH NICKY ... NO WORDS CAN EXPRESS YOUR PAIN AND ANGUISH. NO WORDS WILL EVER EXPRESS THE NIGHT AND DAYS ENDURED BROKEN AND UNEXPRESSED. AS YOU SAID TO ME LAST YEAR, IT'S ALL A SHOW. WE SEE THE SIGHT UNSEEN, HOWEVER, MOMMY SHOWED YOU HOW LIFE IS REAL FROM THE BEGINNING TO THE END WITH EYES WIDE OPEN WITH TRUE UNCONDITIONAL LOVE. FROM THE MOMENT YOU WERE CONCEIVED UNTIL YOU LOOKED UPON MY EYES ON 12/29/2006, I KNOW YOUR TRUTH. A MOTHERS UNCONDITIONAL LOVE WILL NEVER DISSIPATE.

FOREVER YOURS,
YOUR LOVINGLY MOTHER TO THE END,
MOMMY 11/29/2006

YOU AND ME AGAINST THE WORLD, SOMETIMES IT STILL FEELS LIKE YOU AND me against the world, when all the others turn their backs and walk away...a song that never leaves my mind. My phone did not ring once this past Thanksgiving...literally. Not one call. It makes me sick. Now I know why you were so drawn to be around, cause people fed off your goodness. Unfortunately, no one could ever wear your shoes.

Nicky, you are so lucky where you are, free of pain physically and emotionally. You were too good to be here any longer that is why God called you. It is all coming into play as each day and holiday passes. I can't wait to meet you in heaven and leave this place called HELL. I love meeting you in my dreams and being with you every day. Love, Mommy

---

THREE YEARS HAVE PASSED DECEMBER 29,2008

Three Years `Don't they go by in a blink?

BELOW ARE THE WORDS I SPOKE TO MY SON ON HIS FINAL BIRTHDAY WHEN HE turned eighteen years old.

WHAT A GLORIOUS DAY. EVERY FACE I SEE IS A MEMORY. IT MAY NOT BE A perfectly perfect memory. Sometimes we had our ups and downs. But we're all together, and you're my son's for a day. And I'm going to break precedent and tell you my one candle wish: that you would have a life as lucky as mine, where you can wake up one morning and say, "I don't want anything more." 18 years. Don't they go by in a blink?

I loved Nicky from the moment he was born, and I love him now and every minute & breath in between. And what I dream of is today, that Nicky, you will stop worrying about Mommy, our bond is unconditional, I want you to live life every single day with no regrets, just as I have. Sing with rapture and dance like a dervish babe.

Happy Birthday, Nicky, I love you.

I ALSO WANTED TO SAY THESE WORDS TO NICKY BUT NEVER WAS ABLE TO DO SO~ In addition to this dream I wish for you, is to find a woman who will discover you, and that you will discover a woman who will love you, who is worthy of you, who is of this world, this time and has the grace, compassion, and fortitude to walk beside him as he makes her way through this beautiful thing called life.

I AM STILL NUMB BOUND BY THE EMPTINESS OF NOT SEEING YOU WALK through the door with that big smile, and most of all I miss how you kissed me every single time you went to bed or left the house, you never missed a beat. You were so grateful, your heart was huge, you thought of others even in your final moments before God took you home.

This life without you is a struggle, I only have known the very essence of being a mother and to nurture my children. I have grown to learn that people are very selfish ˜yet people come into your life to help us grow to another level˜ our journey here is not easy.

I am peaceful within knowing you are safe and that one day I will meet with you˜I know you are always around me helping me attain the strength I need to get through another day. I talk about you all the time to people I meet ˜I don't cry" I speak with pride about my son. You were everything a mother could wish for˜when I conceived you, I wished & prayed to God every night that you would be remarkable only one of its kind. And you were˜and still are, Nicky, I can endure another day without you as I feel you beside me while I walk a tumultuous path through life˜

Love, Mommy

TODAY IS JUNE 20TH, 2019

Fourteen Years

BEAUTIFUL MINDS INSPIRE OTHERS.

Thanks to all of those who are like-minded and understand the grief journey. For without your support and friendship you are the muse behind my breath.

I am living proof a broken heart can still live. We Will Never Forget You

Where are they now?... I often wonder how life is treating Nicky's friends, most have moved on.

A few have stayed in touch. After all, when you open your heart and home for so many years, especially the night he died... Allowing them to say goodbye... life changes.

Nicky's heart was bigger than most...

Our loss was overwhelming, the letters written were so beautiful. We were and still are devastated.

If you're experiencing tremendous loss in your grief journey, do not despair from the one still living. Bonding together will create a respect of loyalty for the deceased.

Embrace those grieving. Do not leave them behind. Keep in touch. Let them know you care and respect their loved ones.

Written by friend Danielle Vespertino (2016)

"This day, ten whole years ago, this Earth lost a very special and unique individual. Although my time with him personally was much shorter than many others who loved and adored him, he indeed made an irreplaceable mark in my life and spirit. It is because of this person I chose the profession of nursing.

"I was in my first semester of nursing school when Nicky transitioned, and it was through him I pressed on through all of its difficulties, as hard as it was. Most people know I became a nurse at a very young age. I have dealt with many types of situations in my career that doesn't come easy to your average twenty-year-old.

"In tough times, during my professional career, I've thought of Nick and his courage, faith, and perseverance through his most difficult times as an adolescent.

"And then I think to myself. HE dealt with things more difficult than that of your average teenager. I've watched him at his best, and I've seen him at his worst. I've watched him suffer through all the side effects of chemo, and I saw how much it drained him.

"And I also watched him keep his humor and personality through it all. I've also seen him on his best days, making others laugh or laughing with other people, simply enjoying the happiest parts of life.

"To this very day, I have never met a stronger individual

in my life than he. And, as much as I wish he were still here to this very day, making me laugh for hours on end, I know that he was called for a reason: to watch down on us all. I am ever so thankful to have had him as a friend. And I am forever grateful that he has touched my life."

WE ARE PRESSED ON EVERY SIDE BY TROUBLES, BUT WE ARE NOT CRUSHED OR broken. We are perplexed but we won't give up and quit. We are hunted down, but God never abandons us. We get knocked down, but we get back up and keep going.

(Written by Nick Bell...on a sticky note left on his mother's monitor four months before he passed away.)

9 781633 63